# A GARDEN

# OF

# HAPPINESS

# NARAINE DATT

# ACKNOWLEDGEMENTS

This is my fourth book. The first two, *A Lonely Voice*, and **Drink from My Calabash** were my own, while the third, **Roraima,** was co-authored with 5 other poets, all my friends. I hope to continue my partnership with them in the future.

I would like to thank my immediate family for encouraging me to finish this project, as well as my relatives and friends, Savitri Bisessar, Joe Persaud, Bertie Ramcharan, Robert Singh and Adolphus Sukhai.

Poets are like artists in quest of the ideal, with big hearts and a wider canvas to hone their craft. I am at peace when writing poetry, as when I am fishing. Each poem is like watching a child growing up. As it emerges, there is satisfaction in expressing ourselves and we feel at home seeing it take shape. So thanks to all my friends, writers, teachers and folks from my memorable village of Bush Lot, W.C Berbice in my beloved Guyana.

# CONTENTS

## CHAPTER I

## POEMS OF HOPE

## CHAPTER II

## FROM OUR DIASPORA

CHAPTER III

# POLYTRICKS & POLITICS

CHAPTER IV

# THE NEXT CHAPTER

# CHAPTER I

# POEMS OF HOPE

# A GARDEN OF HAPPINESS

*Life is a song - sing it.*
*Life is a game - play it.*
*Life is a challenge - meet it.*
*Life is a dream - realize it.*
*Life is a sacrifice - offer it.*
*Life is love - enjoy it.*
<u>Sai Baba</u>

Close your eyes and imagine your life in as another Eden[1]
And you can call it yours and can build a fence around it
Below the surface there's a system of roots in this garden
Responsibility for the garden's growth will keep you fit
How do you cultivate this garden of happiness?
And what is its impact on the greater whole
Till the soil with compassion without any finesse
Sow your seeds with love and all your soul
Compassion should be you only tool
Your attitude and actions should be kind nothing new
Yes! do remember the Golden Rule,
Do unto others as you would have them do unto you

---

[1] *Remember God was smart when he too started life in the Garden of Eden .*

Love is what we all humans do need and deserve
Love is the power that creates, soothes and heals
Don't get caught in the hidden agendas, just serve
We're all in dire need of love to turn life's wheels
From the need for love no one is born free
So love, give it freely the more we cultivate
Recognizing our interdependence you'll see
The happier we become even with our mate

Make a commitment to treat everyone as an old friend
No matter whom you encounter
Even if the other person is challenging you to the end
No matter if its a foe or a brother
See them as an opportunity to be kind for seven days

Educate yourself with animals slaughtered cruelly
Don't only practice man's compassion in abysmal ways
See animals killed for food are treated humanely
All of life deserved to be free from suffering
Eat less meat and consider a plant-based diet
Love all living things with kindness and caring
Try taking the bug you find on the floor outside
Instead of squatting it, you may surprise
How different you would feel especially inside
You'll feel good like just won a big prize

Do not be content with trifle feelings or needs
All is not well if you just sit on your housetop
In your garden you have to get rid of the weeds
So do not sit back waiting to reap your crop

Nurture your heart grow some flowers
To attract the insects to pollinate your tomatoes
Even when it rains respect the showers
Watch out for the squirrels and other's burrows
Like mulching get rid of petty jealousies
And smell the roses and breathe in pure fresh air
You may lose from the pickings of birdies
But your life would be better for whom you care

# MOTHERS

Without mothers we surely won't be here
It's fitting to celebrate one day of the year
But after being motherly for 365 days
We really should show it in more ways
For these beautiful people mothers
Who're our aunts, wives and sisters
Our over worked nurses, and doctors
Our friends and everyday teachers
Yet in some places of this planet
Not a tiny respect they don't get
They are abused and denied their right
And stopping this wrong is not in sight
Mothers are very precious
Their meals are delicious
For the socks or shirt you cannot find
A mother is there to soothe your mind
If you are lazy and leave your room in a mess
She'll fret but she'll clean it I have to confess
Some kids' eyes are covered with wool
Then motherhood to them is ungrateful
They love you with faults anyhow
They will even face a butting cow
If someone ever threaten a mother's young
Even if you threaten to cut out their tongue
They will defend their young so gallantly

And you will always have their loyalty
They are the bulwark of the health systems
They're more precious than diamond or gems
No matter how warring with flags we unfurled
Our loving mothers brought us into this world

# IT'S NOT WORTH IT

How many times we've heard this after the fact
When the user showed no common sense or tact
How many times you heard this sound
The culprit wishing he was drowned
When offered the stick or carrot
But **bad company** said the parrot

Looking back it's not worth it
For you always end up in a pit
With buddies when you meet
Maybe it's not all skin teeth
For the next thing **bam!**
You get yourself in a jam

Remember when you sneer and scoff
At others who say you're a chip off
The old block and never fly far
As you sport in a **borrowed** car
You gamble and deal high aces
Now the cops are in your faces

As you take your drugs for your kicks
Knowing you'd be one of the addicts

Using your position flying high
Never breathing a decent sigh
You're darn happy scamming the weak
Forgetting one day you may have a leak

On your backs you carry this immoral load
Deep in your mind it's like a biting sword
For all the ill-gotten gains you've produced
One day the chicken'll come home to roost
I say it again it's not worth it my friend
It will surely bring you down in the end

You have to remember
My lost prodigal brother
Careful when one gives a favour
It all boils down to honest labour
For even when you're in a real crunch
There is no such thing as a free lunch

# LOVE THEM NOW

Don't give them any sorrow
By loving them tomorrow
Those folks around you
And those far away too
Let your heart allow
You to love them now
They are your loving parent
Even when they rave and vent
Or they're your beloved grands
Sometimes making big demands
Your only one for you can't get another
And that is your forever loving mother
Or your daddy, papa or father
And being the sole breadwinner
Sometimes he makes it hard for you to choose
When he's telling you to mind your *ps* and *qs*
But you know that *ol' man* loves you to death
And he will move mountains for you, you bet
Or even a good real brother
Who can be a bloody bother
Or a lil' witch for a sinister sister
As you are tempted to choke her
But the next minute she's your treasure
Even with her hiccups as you tease her
Or maybe one of your aunts

Though she wears the pants
Looking at her in a very different slant
When you say can and she says can't
Maybe an old kind Uncle
With his hands so wrinkle
And not forgetting the people
Though you may consider evil

Be nice to appease that officer
Who put you in a homely shelter
Who gave you that heavy mortgage
Even with O.T.$^2$.now feeling the edge
And the humorous barber
Yeah how he can chatter
But he keeps you shyly smiling
As his scissors do the cutting
And your little old shoemaker
Your one and only sole taker

The time your beloved smiled that memorable day
You're comfuffled cause you forgot her birthday
And was wondering how to rectify this
But you were saved by the able florist
So next time on your trip you pass by her shop
A thank you note in an envelope you can drop

These and many more are the folks
Who are there for us busy blokes

---

² *OT is over-time*

And your car like a kitten is purring
'cause of your mechanic's engineering

And then there's your old family doctor
Maybe brought forth your sis or brother
Sometimes a bit busy to mind his bedside manner
Remember the angina when he repaired your ticker
Now you may live yet another decade
Until you've another serious escapade

What of your buddy and bosom friends
Who may sometimes behave like fiends
They are the people who grew up with you
Massaging your ego when times were blue

And then there are your now and then teachers
Who may at sometimes sounds like preachers
You may go further and call them creatures
That's why you love all kinds of literatures

And what about the writer and authors
Who wrote about princes and about curs
How they make you alive all those years
When their books brought such long tears
To your sorry eyes giving you renewed strength
Allowing you to set your standards to any length

And our brave soldiers so far
Fighting in Afghanistan's war
Leaving at home their loved ones

Living by loving emails in tons
Battling bullets and suicide bombers
Fighting evil in their crescent towers
Who are preserving our freedom
As politicians nitpicking so dumb

So if we stop fret, fuss and vent
Abide by this one commandment
We can change the worl'
With only one flag to twirl
Don't give them any sorrow
By loving them tomorrow
Let your heart do allow
Go ahead love them now

# DREAMS DO COME THROUGH

Me think I remember a poem which says
Sleep to dream or dream to sleep!
I say dreams come through in many ways
Especially when your sleep is deep
It can happen even to the simple fellow
To shorten that eastern passage around Africa
Many had dreams including Marco Polo
Who founded the desired **Silk Road to China**

Even braver was Christopher Columbus
He had to cross the stormy oceans for sure
There is some who still fret and make fuss
That **Amerigo Vespucci** did it long before
He thought he was going east with the nice breeze
But he ended up in the West sailing Santa Maria
And **discovered**[1] America and the West Indies
Followed by his other ships the Pinta and Nina

Long! long before all of them
Cornered by the malicious army of Egyptians
Moses had the biggest problem
Parting the seas to escape those cruel Romans
Some producers of modern Hollywood
Put the Ten Commandments on film

---

[1] *The jury is still out there that Amerigo Vespucci discovered
America before Christopher Columbus and it was named after him.*

Made our dreams came true so we could
All witness the mighty power of **Him**

Not long ago a simple ***naked fakir***[2] of India
Mohandas Gandhi had a giant of a dream
To gain Independence with ***Satyagrah***[3]
Making a united India with his dream team
But religion can be so bad sometimes
Nehru and Gandhi wanted one India
Men can become real snakes in slimes
Jinnah wanted a Pakistani nation
Despite Nehru's and Gandhi's pleas at par
Jinnah still clamored for partition
Resulting with the two nations still at war

Followers of Gandhi like the Rev. King
Dreamt of peace with the two races
The Rev. Martin Luther King had the sting
Despite all the bigoted racial menaces
The blacks and whites finally came together
This dream was cemented by Barak Obama
They thought they'd never see a black brother
Occupying the White House in America

Once the only British country in South America
Dr Cheddi Jagan's dreams came through partly

---

[2] Sir Winston Churchill called Gandhi a ***naked fakir***

[3] ***Satyagrah*** is the Hindi word for ***Non Violence***

Making a people with one destiny in Guyana
'though he was jailed at Sibley Hall wrongfully
By LFS Burnham who was once his pal
And for 28 years was sabotaged politically
Eventually the dictator Burnham did fall
And Dr. Jagan again won democratically

A man waited in jail in Robben Island
And for 28 years he dreamt of freedom
Through global intervention's demand
Eventually his bloody release did come
For black South Africans the majority
Then Mandela took power anew
Casting aside the white ruled minority
And many dreams came through

In Canada's we had a peculiar dish
Dreams of the French Quebecois united
With all the peace loving English
A peace Pierre Trudeau did cemented
Bringing home the constitution
Despite the attempt of Dief our Chief
Stopping the Quebec's separation
Got all under the flag of the maple leaf

The greatest woman with a mountain of strength
The indomitable modern day Saint Mother Teresa
Whose charity touched India's width and length
Resulting in building her **Peace Village** in India
Where others, Hindus and Muslims came

She was rewarded with the Noble Peace Prize
For feeding the sick, the poor and the lame

Dreams came through for millions not long ago
When Obama became president of the USA
This was very impossible many thought so
Where the colour barrier held many at bay
This cause inspiration to heighten
A real black man in the Whitehouse finally
Planting his own vegetable garden
Building self esteem to downtrodden globally

Every year students fulfill their dreams
At graduation time tossing their hats in the air
Hoping for betterment or so it seems
Like their parents hoping to get their share
Addicted alcoholics have dreams too
Suffering and living one day at a time
So are the smokers which is nothing new
As they continue to cough up slime

Fishermen go to sea and cast their nets
Hoping today they'll catch the big one
Addicted gamblers also cast their bets
Stupidly thinking they are having fun
Some folks in Sri Lankha and Darfur
Have simple dreams of finding food and shelter
Their crime is that they are so poor
As warlords having them running helter skelter

And on the sidelines the wolves stand
They too have dreams of their own
A fat strayed calf is their demand
As they listen for its motherly moan
The anteater too dream with it's sticky tongue
Looking for a nice juicy packed ant-hill
Silently moving up a mound without a sound
Today he may get his dreams and his fill

As they too endlessly search near and far
Helping the crops of the farmers thrive
The bees dream of flowers to gather nectar
As they busily make honey in their hive
And as the full of dreams world goes on
All hope one day theirs too may come through
Some would win and some die and gone
Some will be happy and some would be blue

# GIVE PEACE ANOTHER CHANCE

Again we're on the brink
And we may not sink
But we cease to think
Because of our past link

What is it that makes man
Hate another man
With so much venom
We can hardly fathom

Is it fear of the unexpected
That make them so dejected
That they would kill
Using all their skill

Is it just to keep going
Their machine producing
Machinations of destruction
Against other warring nation

The so-called peace maker
Is not quite a real qualifier
For she sat by unrelented
As'r own were maltreated

She went around the world so hot
And doing good or so she thought
Yet all her good deeds
Cocooned in bad seeds

If we cannot learn from history
The media will get another story
Until some other evil bigger bully
Continue with an entry very ugly

All the billions spent on war
Can be used and will go far
Against the catalysts of this predicament
Destroying a beautiful blue environment

Yes man! declare war against poverty
The homeless, landless and child slavery
Hunger, corruption, nepotism and crime
The drug lords, warlords and other slime

And warmongers listen to the women
Who are treated like cattle by men
If only man can give peace another chance
Can you imagine the very sweet new dance

We can have everyone without fear
Holding hands in unity and prayer
But and if we continue like this
We're going to run out of bliss

# MONEY IS NOT EVERYTHING

I was grown up in a humble home
I which we had no time to roam
Now looking back we were poor
And I didn't miss much for sure
I had no father to turn to or trus'
He scared the hell of all 5 of us
Around him we walked as on eggshell
For he was always so serious and cruel
Glad always to go to our Uncles' visits
56 miles away but we got love and bits[1]
Their love to us was great and was new
And also all the things good fathers do
When holidays were over they would send
Us back home though reluctantly in the end
We left our good Uncles with toys and money
Wishing one of them would adopt me eventually

It did happen afterwards though
She later knew it was time to go
When things got really bereft
She said that's **enough** and left

---

[1] *In those days being British, we used the English money (Pound, shilling and pence) and a bit was valued at about 8 cents.*

But although poverty was our crime
We took it in tune and bid our time
I'm thankful to my mother who did her best
Urging us to do get high marks in every test
To get energy she would gave us her breakfast
For our daily 5mile walk to school, thus we last
She did her best doing menial chores alone
For her in-laws who worked her to the bone

Good manners we inherited from our birth
Like saying **Good Morning** with all its worth
**Thank you** when you receive something
Politely smile to people in your greeting
Before you enter a home take your hat off your head
Also shoes off for sure especially when you go to bed
On waking up make up your bed and tidy your room
Brush your teeth after every meal  be well groomed
Never ever let the rising sun catch you in bed asleep
You are in big trouble with your parents for our keep

So when I came to North America
Then eventually to good ol'Canada
I was shocked, all the mannerisms we were taught
The folks here forsook all and turned it to naught
Was ignored by the Caucasians
Which also include the Canadians
I saw nice women smoking and driving
Using make-up and on their cells talking
With their kids in their vans or cars
Women flirting and drinking at bars

26

Women swearing and dress so shabbily
To me it was a sad disappointing society
Even pregnant women imbibing at dances
And taking so many precarious chances
In their high 6" heels and almost new born
With hangovers the next day all so forlorn
Shamefully like lushes as they left exposing
Themselves to diseases as they all cavorting

Some do anything to get cash
Or to feed their vices with hash
From the ridiculous to all most going nude
With back talk and behaving so very rude
Children liming about in every mall
Without any adult  supervision at all
At late hours with their clique or gangs
Too busy snorting amidst unkempt bangs

Drinking mixing and smoking
Just like their parents are doing
The future of the nations
Despite all your stations
I looked upon this so-called civilized society
I think my mother did a good job darn pretty
And its proof of the pudding
That money is not everything

# WHY I'M HAPPY

I'm happy for once knowing my grandmother
And growing up with a kind and loving mother
I married my loving wife and even now
I knew what real joy you is guess how!
I was very happy when I got my two sons
Very far from fetching water by gallons
I'm happy knowing my aunts and uncles
We're happy even without gold or bangles
I am happy living firstly at Nabaclis village
Although t'was like living in real bondage
Moving to the village of Bush Lot
In a place where I was a have-not
Where I made and still have some good friends
We made bush-cooks on memorable weekends
I was very happy to get my first job *bhaya*
Although it was far away at Anna Regina
Knew some real buddy friends very loving folks
Far from home traded cokes for some smokes
I was making and saving my own money
And that my friend made me very happy
I'm happy when I am with Nature listening
To birds chirping very early in the morning
To be awoken by the crowing of the cock
And the rumblings of the nearby livestock
Sweet songs of doves and singing thrushes
Perched somewhere in some dense bushes

And I feel peaceful when I'm near water
Maybe I was once a different creature
People look at trees and bushes and miss the scene
I see the myriads of hues of blues, reds and green
Enjoy scenes of hanging clouds o'r distant mountains
These gems are free to all for less than most bargains
I'm awed at a scene of a sinking sunset
This is a memory you'd never forget
And you may think I am insane
But I do love to walk in the rain
I love to feel this sense I inherited from birth
Getting my hands deep down in Mother Earth
Watching my kitchen plants thrive
Talking and caring for them so alive
I'm especially happy writing poetry
Trying to be in sync with my country
I feel happy and fruitful when I'm finished
Maybe to be read or not even to be published
I look at each poem like a new child
Like others some are tame others wild
Seeing a good movie that is worthwhile
Especially when it makes me sob or smile
And lying on the grass by a bubbling brook
I'm very happy when reading a good book
Especially one of espionage and intrigue
Sometimes reaching far above my league
Yes and I'm happy to watch
Evil doers meet their match
How they're repaid when they steal from the poor
As karma comes biting their asses for an encore

I'm happy I lived in  peaceful beautiful Canada
Enjoying a peace of mind I never had in Guyana
Doing good for others makes me really happy
When there's a mixture of hope and charity

# YOU'RE NEVER LONELY WITH GOOD FRIENDS

How many times we see on TV the other side
One from a family who just committed suicide
'cause he'd been bullied not as a suicide bomber
As we close the coffin and return to our computer

We question and lay blame on the government
We are too scared helpless and cannot be blunt
Then we try to enforce new laws by ourselves
Hoping the answer is found from the shelves

They had good intentions who begat this social network
If and when it is used ethically even just for schoolwork
But teenage girls behaving like crows with a carcass
By bullying the weak and the least educated in class

Not to be outdone boys on busses act so macho
It's as if self respecting teenage lads gone loco
Stand-bys are just as guilty as these brainless culprits
One wonders were they picked up these heinous habits

They're afraid to talk to parents who'd just brush them off
Stuck in cocoons with cell phones as if they have a cough

But they have no good friends for they never made any
Their efforts maybe thwarted by some batty creepy bully

Parental guidance is severed as with a knife
To stay the mortgage or other expenses of life
Kids left alone feel lonely and locked in a vise
The effect is the loved ones pay a bitter price

Withdrawn daily staying indoors playing games
On line every darn minute chatting without aims
Getting fat on just pure unadulterated trash
When caught they changed tunes in a flash

It all boils down to the family who eats together
They're more caring for kids are a real treasure
When they can talk openly about life and school
Work, stop the bullying not becoming a footstool

And they will stand fast by you to the end
They won't offend or pretend but defend
And you all would look out for one another
For keeping close good friends are forever

# NEVER BE ASHAMED OF YOUR FAMILY

Even the greats never see the light
And not everything came out right
Some were outcasts and rejects
History is filled with such texts
With the damn and the ashamed
Is God the one to be blamed?
And behaved like a real jerk
Some hell bent went berserk

Deranged psychologically may be
But they are all yours for eternity
Sometime they are sad sometime happy
Some may call them downright barmy
When you look at them you see family
Written all over their faces so happy
Because of them you can strive
And you are very glad to be alive

In all forms refusing to confirm
Some maybe even darn deformed
But they belong to your family
Learn to live with them lovingly
To you they belonged to your crowd
So lift your shoulder and walk proud

To you and yours it does not matter
For blood is way thicker than water

# I'M TOO BLESSED TO BE STRESSED

I thought I was lucky and very blessed
So  I looked back at the life I caressed
All those who gave me a hard time
They gave me rings for my chime
It came from mostly from people I know
But their pessimism propelled me to go
And I laughed at them so puerile
Made note and put into my file
It boils down to not having love
Even better for the One above
For themselves and their brothers
How can they really love others
They each have a warped mind
With small brains so confined
They thought they have the cure
This burden makes them impure
And I really feel so good as I smile
To know I'm a winner all the while
You see me too is very blessed
That is why I am not stressed
And you ask how do I look at life
Prefer those who don't make strife

Those who are simple and contented
Not materially obsessed or demented
Not those thinking how to out do another
Or trying to con or to hoodwink a brother

To me they are just a bag of waste
Folks who I would never embrace
So you see how I'm out of that mess
Its because I'm so thankfully blessed

# I'M GOING TO WALK OUT OF THIS JUNGLE

It sounds simple but it was stupid
And I blamed no one for what I did
I went up North with buddies of mine
To spend a few days and all was fine

We reached Tory Hill around eight o'clock
We looked around then we curried the duck
Later we had a few drinks and went to bed
Not knowing in a few hours I could be dead

The next day we visited some friends nearby
We played cards late then had some shut-eye
Whats the problem *so far your story looks glum*
I know what you're saying there's more to come

We settled down and retired or so I assume
I remembered heading for the washroom
Then **Bam!** I was in this **strange** cottage
I heard some snoring as I passed a passage

Trying to find the door was not easy
Not wanting to wake up **this** family
I found the door and exited silently
I crept out of that house stealthily

I ran out side not wanting to be caught
Looking for our cottage or so I thought
Into the bushes in my bare socks I ran
Over sticks snows faster than batman

It was a dark jungle bordered with fright
Especially about ten o'clock in the night
It was about ten below zero without a coat
Wishing to hear even the sound of a goat

I ended up in a deep valley with huge trees
In panic I cried for **help!** in the cold breeze
I called out to all plodding in the sinking sods
To **Teddy! Jai!** to **my God!** and the other gods

Willing even to provoke an animal's growl
No one answered but dogs started to howl[3]
My socks and pants got iced together
It got worse as I waded through water

---

[3] *Dogs have a remarkable sense of hearing, they heard me but their barkings were quickly silenced by their owner who apparently couldn't find or hear anything.*

It got numbed I lost all feelings in my feet
This is crazy as I dispel all signs of defeat
The edge of my walking stick cutting into my palm
Too frozen to feel I couldn't panic had to stay calm


I pushed on asking my Guardian angle
***Show me how to walk out of this jungle***
Even if it kills me I was getting tired and weary
Realizing I can die here and no one will find me


A lot of things went through my mind and head
What I would not give for a warm floor or bed
The onus was on me to find a way out of here
I know surely help have to be somewhere near


Who'd remember me if I am not here any longer
I did a good job with my family they'd remember
I never get to enjoy even my absent grands
I was easy going never making demands


Once in a man's life he should be subjected
By being lost to see the life he has created
Now money meant nothing only warmth
A strong drink, a good fire near a hearth


I fell backwards climbing over some wood
I laid in the snow and said maybe I should
Stay here and wait for the search team
Go to sleep and this is all a bad dream

I was cold now dying at my not so old age
Too stupid to run out of that warm cottage

To get lost in the middle of this nearby forest
Trying to live a good life and got in this mess

Then something made me stood up and I panted
***"I am gonna walk out of the jungle",*** I shouted
I started to walk and then I saw a light
I knew my angel was leading me right

Such feelings come as **when a kid sees Santa**
Or to witness **a first child held by his father**
Maybe after two to three hours I can't recall
I approached a cottage now gutsy with gall

I saw that road and with my iced feet I walked home
To my friend's cottage gladly to say **hello** or **shalom**
I was freezing as they piled blankets on my bosom
And I started to tremble thinking about the outcome

Today I looked at life through different lens
With my very few foes I'll make all amends
Respect for nature and eternal love for angels
And promise to stay afar from all tall jungles

# EDUCATE YOUR HEART

Once when you were young you went to school
Your good parents thought you were not a fool
From Kindergarten to Harvard maybe
Without a scar entering life's society
Empty pockets never held anyone back.
Only empty heads will take up the slack
Speak from the heart people will listen
A loving heart will in wisdom glisten
Blessed hearts bend never break always be fit
But if you can't put your heart in it get out of it

A woman's head is always influenced by her heart
But a man's heart is always influenced by his head
Follow your inner heart it helps and the world moves in
And be true to yourself your bosom will be without sin
Knock and ask your heart what it doth know
It'll beat in the rhythm in music not for show
How much the heart can really hold no one knows
For at any age it has no wrinkles and it never shows
The way to God is through a human heart for a start
For all music is important if it comes from the heart

Remember how happy you were meek and mild
'cause your heart was pure and simple as a child
Why is peace, grace and contentment come to some
If you've inner awareness a grateful heart will come
Look at every path closely and deliberately
Try it as many times as you think necessary
Ask yourself, this question and yourself alone
Does this path have a heart or a good tone?
If it does, then the path is good.
If it doesn't, it's like rotten wood

They teach how to get results in your exams
Some are honest but some resort to scams
Many teachers don't teach you life sense
Especially if you appear somewhat dense
You are left with nice rainbows in your head
As you watch the boob tube until you're red
They put the cart before the donkey
And throw you in a murky society
But whenever or before you ever depart
They should've tried to educate your heart

# THE BLESSINGS OF THY FATHERS

Well aren't you better off than your homeland brothers
And better yet than your own fathers and your mothers
What blessings you may ask
Well that's not too hard a task
In India, Africa, China or southeast Asia
Even good old Europe or far off Guyana
Most of you have your own car, land or a fridge
A house with mown lawn with a wide frontage
And maybe some dollars in your bank account
And even a pony or horse in a stable to mount
For you're the products of a very proud heritage
And real honest pioneers who showed courage

Those who toiled today can show the results
In peace far from violence and nasty insults
When some tried to pray to Ram or Allah

Or to return to the Motherland of India
They were also struck dumb when they landed
Since then Motherlands aren't being demanded
Really! could this were where we yearned to go
The squalor, filth and poverty gave us a big blow
The caste system, and women's maltreatment
An ancient way of life so hideously indecent
Very shocking and disappointed we returned home
With thanks to our forefathers who left that dome

As many in America still complaining woefully
After 175 years about not given the opportunity
Still suffocating in food stamps and steep in welfare
Others are scraping and crawling to come over here
They're still blaming Caucasians for their freedom
As others risk deadly shark infested waters to come
And other immigrants just came over within decades
Doing the menial chores in farms, kitchens and maids
And they have risen above the standards of the natives
Who are still stewing over same old same old motives
Have they forgotten how their forefathers denied entry

To Sikhs[4],Jews[5],Haitians and folks from other ancestry?

Then the other motherland Africa still struggling
Blaming the west and others for their suffering
Her politicians and leaders forever in tribal warfare
Invade, defy, doing what they want without any care
As new leaders on the other side use machetes
Wiping out the opposition and also old cronies
Like toppled Somalia in warlordism and mass butchery
As little babies and women cry out like wailing banshee
Murder rampages of bewigged young men in Liberia

---

Ethnic genocide killings across the border in Rawanda
Dumping their corpses into the Kagera River hard to find
Or into Lake Victoria, out of sight, better yet out of mind.

The USA running around in the name of democracy
Warring against anti this and that in every darn alley
Righting the wrongs or so they thought
Until they were ousted or were caught
Being branded the villain and infidel by some
Who never know the meaning of real freedom
But prolifcation of the west came from their motherland
Resulting in conquering every acre of Red Indian's land
Then came karma back to bite them elsewhere
Now left with warfare and steeped in welfare
At the same time preaching about their dying constitution
Sandwiched between the Second Amendment and Goshen

# CHAPTER II

# FROM OUR DIASPORA

1. **I AM A COOLIE** *(The Pioneers)*
2. **MY GUYANA** *(The Paradise)*
3. **MY GUYANA** (*The Land of Six Peoples*)
4. **MY GUYANESE**
5. **AN ADDENDUM TO MY GUYANA**
6. **A GUYANESE XMAS**
7. **THE LOADED DUNGS TREE** *(The Dead Donkey)*
8. **MY BLOOD IS IN YOUR SUGAR**
9. **REMEMBER WISMAR**
10. **THE NON PARIEL UPRISING**
11. **BECHU**
12. **THE CHILDREN OF THE JAHAJIS**
13. **THE CANE CUTTER**
14. **DOWN BY THE SEASIDE**
15. **THE SEA WALL**

*The ignorant mind, with its infinite afflictions, passions, and evils, is rooted in the three poisons. Greed, anger, and delusion.*
**Bodhidharma**

# I AM A COOLIE
## (The Pioneers)

As stated before then
I went in the coolie den
There wouldn't have been any Guyana
Without any coolies from Mother India
Our dharma is the best in the world
Made us as others' bloods curled
Very proud coolies in that clime
Our forefathers had a rough time
From Brahmins to Musahar
Chatris and Madrassies so far
They came bare without luggage
They left all their bias baggage
When they boarded the ships
But they made lasting kinships
Yes they have become *jahajis*[6]
Thank the Lord they did this

---

[6] *These pioneers who came from Mother India*
*Are the East Indians today with a proud dharma*
*That's still practiced with vigor and zest*
*For they had the stamina to come West*
**THE JAHAJIS by Naraine Datt**

They've passed on their robust genes
And have developed unique cuisines
Good **broughtupsy** and **etiquette**
Maybe it was ordained as **kismet**
Some call it discipline or **broad leather**
Knock heads, bramble licks Oh brother!
Also known as **cut rass**
Which you get in class
We did not need anyone to teach us about the truth
Respect for other people's property and being couth
We went to school to learn
Listen to our teachers
Not to yap on the phone
Or to moan and groan
Not to play video games
But focus and have aims
Not to disrupt classes
Like confound asses
From birth we were keen
About personal hygiene
Our parents took very much care
With inevitable clean underwear
Wash your face and at a very early age
Brushing teeth even if its with black sage
Wash your hands before you eat
And after you touch the toilet seat
And take your shoes off on entering
Never wear them to bed go sleeping
Cover your mouth
When you cough

It was a way of life
And talk about being thrift
You never ever spend
What you don't have
If you can't buy it for cash
Then wait until you can

We build our houses
Then we built our homes
Sometimes we make do
Living with parents
We never owe the banks
Later on we say thanks
To our coolie parents
And so we're never caught
In any financial quagmire

We've become the best
Having the coolies
Spending their last cent
Educating their children
We've built villages and cities
Which stand out from the rest
We became linguists
Learning English, Hindi
Urdhu and Patwa

We still sing our old time songs
Play the harmonium and dhantal
Dance when the tassa drums call

Belt out our chatneys
At social gatherings
And live our life to suit us
As others make a lot of fuss
We belong to various faiths
Hindus, Muslims, Christians
We celebrate all holidays
We pray for Eid
Get ready for Christmas
And can't wait for Phagwah

The Hindu temple
Sits near the Mosque
Overlooking the Church
The coolies around the world
Can show other nations
How to live in peace

# MY GUYANA

### (The Paradise)

My Guyana was a real Paradise
When I left in nineteen seventy
Everything was sugar and spice
The people were free and happy

My Guyana was of real unity
People working and living together
Not one of hatred or of enmity
Setting one race against the other

My Guyana was a real Paradise
What I saw when I visited I became very sick
Nothing was good, safe, or nice
Not what was said when we became a Republic

The Botanic Gardens one of Guyana's pride
Also the Museum, the Zoo for visitors and all to see
Not a haven for the choke and robbers to hide
But where Queen Victoria presided in all her majesty

Stabroek market was a real busy hive of activity
Happy banter, bargaining and music filled the streets
Everywhere there was love, life, laughter and gaiety
And the vendors' stands filled with greens and sweets

It was when our dholl was a staple food
When the people eat what and when they wish
Not banning an item when in a racial mood
And there is no substitute for a similar dish

My Guyana has no earthquakes or hurricanes
Cyclones, volcanoes or winters
Except at times a few rough tides on the main
Cool perpetual 75 degree summers

My Guyana was the hub of the West Indies
Exporting to the main and all the Islands
To North America, Europe and across the seas
And kept up with all the numerous demands

Rice was top and sugar was still  King then
Guyana was famous for its long grain Super rice
And #79 rice was far better than Uncle Ben
The labours and result of all the farmers' sacrifice

The East Indians are the farmers of Guyana
The sweat of their brows feed the nation
From the sweet sugar-cane to the long bora
Fruits of good husbandry and dedication

The Indians came and became very prosperous
After emancipation the Negroes left the main
My forefathers came in the ship the **Hesperus**
To work on the plantations cutting cane

From Crabwood Creek to the distant Point Playa
The 270 mile long coastland was the country
That is what I remember of my beautiful Guyana
In '83 that is what I would have liked to see

Instead, my humble heart bled everyday
To see my beloved country in pain dying
A shanty town, shocked to see it this way
Stifled by the ever present army patrolling

I found a ghetto instead of Georgetown
The fear and decay were everywhere
Which would scare even a hog or hound
Neither would want to stay or live there

Black Market was the way of life
The prices were so darn bloody high
All around was teeming with strife
You watch the goods but cannot buy

In Guyana there are two laws
Black marketing for us was illegal
Party members have no flaws
If caught it is your own downfall

The PM said you can never join the band
You had to be born in it
They want to change the face of the land
Another slogan by that misfit

Grants and aids were divided
Given to the army and supporters' purse
As the state's coffers subsided
Making the PNC government a curse

Like maggots eating away among the ranks
Licking the platter leaving the treasury bare
Stacking it away in some foreign banks
Always asking the taxpayer further to share

The Government now masters of divide and rule
Has turned friend into foe, son against father
Convincingly using this cheap low trick as a tool
To keep the peoples at war so they stay in power

The party wants to change your pigmentation
National Service, a guise to corrupt our women
To blend them gradually into their population
Against the will of the parents, children or men

In my Guyana I remember when you could
Leave your door open without a bother
Cause the people were decent and good
And they always look out for one another

Today Guyana has reached a ridiculous stage
All the houses in the rural countryside
Have design iron bars resembling a bird cage
Sometimes offering no protection to hide
They would attack anytime day or night
Using anything even the army machine gun
The police or army is never in sight
Always appearing when the damage is done

When your doors and windows are too secure
And they can't kick it down with their army hoof
You're still not safe whether you're rich or poor
For they may be coming through your roof

My Guyana belong to Guyanese at home and abroad
Not fakes elite who usurped power by propagating fears
By violence, rigged ballots making elections  a fraud
But to the punters and the cane cutters, the real pioneers

Now the plane is filled with hucksters
Grabbing goods and items of all types
Forcing off the legitimate passengers
Behaving like wild hyenas with stripes

To clean up the damage of decades of decadence
Even when the darn satanic corrupters are gone
Would call for feats of fortitude and real patience
Hoping to God the old bad blood would pass on

For dictators of yesteryear like Amin
Have gone into hiding or are always on the run
Cause lies and corruption can never win
That's always the end of every son-of-a-gun[7]

---

7 *My Guyana was written in 1983 after I returned from a visit to my beloved Guyana.*

# MY GUYANA
## *(Land of Six peoples)*

The *land of many waters* is *my forever* **Guyana**
Sandwiched between big Brazil and Venezuela
Also called the *land of six peoples*
Although some behave like weevils
Including the Blacks and Indians
And our neglected Amerindians
We live on the flat coastlands
From Point Playa to Springlands
Mesmerized by racial politics
Still using the race card tricks
It appears as if we have a *curse*
With some of us stuck in reverse
Just to stay sober and keep alive
Whilst some are in forward drive
Some myopic and so stubborn
Some hope for newborn morn

My Guyana is Raleigh, Sir Walter
The fearless Elizabethan explorer
He sailed up the Orinoco

Hoping to find **El Dorado**
Around campfires his saga is told
How he came looking for our gold
Dr.Walter Rodney is in My Guyana
The stalwart historian, and teacher
He cleansed their eyes of much **boo-boo**
And on Bent Street he met his Waterloo

My Guyana is Cheddi Jagan
Who showed the world he can
After 28 years in the opposition
To the infamous **Machiavellian**
He found peace and sanity
And brought back democracy
Eventually we got independence
After bitter struggle so immense
With Forbes Burnham the dictator
Who became our misguided leader
I'm somewhat thankful to that **kabaka**
When I couldn't stand the pressure
I left Guyana and came to the USA
And then later settled in Canada

My friends are from all races but not cowards
I judge a man not by his creed but by his words
Not by his racial polytricks
But by his actions and antics
I'm getting there actually but I know
One day I will live to see our show
When Guyanese think like me

Not as a black or a damn coolie
But as one nation with one destiny
Living in sweet peace and harmony

# MY GUYANESE

My Guyana is cricket also man!
With Basil Butcher and Soloman
The star batsmen from Berbice
When Guyana was at real peace
Rohan Kanhai in cricket held the spot
With his famous *falling hook* shot
Who sometimes unfortunately ran out of luck
An overnight's batsman got bowled for a duck
This wasn't for his fans a very good scene
Much to the chagrin of the whole Corentyne
My Guyana is Ted Brathwaite as a teacher
With his novel, *To Sir with Love* as a writer
Sydney Poitiers' portrayal of kids bad and loud
Ted's English experience made us very proud

It also includes J W Chinapen teacher and artist
His poems, *Albion Wilds* at that time was the best
And not forgetting the late great dynamic
Revealing to us of politicians so slick
He turned the darkness into light
Martin Carter's poems were right
With his *Poems of Resistance* so powerful
Uniting a people and making it so crystal

Who literally planted the struggle and need
To fight bad politics, racialism and greed

My Guyana is honored to have great boons
The likes of the lordly Cedric Vernon Nunes
And the wisdom of the late J R Butchey
Teacher and councilor with humility
Philip Moore our famous artist
His art was on all visitor's list
With his **art and sculpture** so unique
Making Guyana reached its peak

What would Guyana be great Scot!
J R Chinapen how can we forgot
The Daybydeens, Bhagwandin a fine man
Indomitable A J Seymour, Clem Seecharan
Nesbit Changur country western singer
Whose **Tain the Beginning** a bestseller
Made us laugh and cry some in shock
That we're alive through all that havoc

So when you are being political
Sowing seeds of distrust so hateful
Joining the highbrows helping
To divide us and keep on ruling
Know ye well! fellow man we are
Good peoples we don't think of war
Living in small towns and tiny villages
Enjoying the same salty sea breezes

Once never divided living like chums
Not by race or politics or by hoodlums

My Guyana is for all the six major races
The Amerindians who made the first traces
The sons and daughters of the blacks
Who came after camouflaged attacks
Of the slaves uprooted from Africa
To build the plantations of the bakrah
And the East Indians shipped from India
These are the people who made Guyana
These coolies really deserve our cheers
What it is today built by these pioneers
And they all have a democratic right
To govern peacefully in their plight

In my Guyana you positively move forward
Throw off your shackles keep up your guard
Stop and think not of the race card game
And neither the old ever blame game
About the past we can't do anything
But from it we can learn something
Take the good dump the negative
And move forward think positive!
Like when we were British Guiana
When we fought the bad bakrah
We thought bad things would cease
And all the races would live in peace
When all the religions were respected
Not where some men were subjected

When we all used to work together
Played and laughed with one another
And sometimes loved each other
Yes that's my kind of Guyana

My Guyana belongs to the farmers
The cane cutters and pork knockers
Even the contentious civil servants
The able policeman and the good soldiers
Firemen, road gangs, pupils and teachers

My Guyana is not for the choke and robbers
Or not some lackadaisical breeders of cancers
Citizens are crying in queues  in this broil
Eking out a living with the hustle and toil
Wearing fat gold chains on their chests
And mocking proudly resisting arrests

My Guyana has no place for ideological asses
Far removed from the welfare of the masses
Bureaucratic hypocritical pencil pushers
And streams of no good paper shufflers
Partying or being entertained by voodoos
And about real practical life has no clues

I'm Guyanese and love me duff and cassava
I was born at Nabaclis village in Demerara
Lived in the beautiful Province of Berbice
And I still relish my black-eye rice and peas

And still love my juicy Buxton spice mango
Firstly worked at Anna Regina in Essequibo

I seldom complain and or fret
And damn proud of it you bet
My Grandfather's bones are sadly buried
Very far from where he once got married
There he died searching for gold
Seeking a better life for his fold
In the heartland of the rough Kurupung region
Where he did and made his final gold bastion

My great great grandfather, a seer
Was a prince from rich Kashmir
I'm a real Brahmin by birth
But I fly low near the earth
I'm getting there actually I know
One day I will live to see our show
When Guyanese think like me
Not as a black or a damn coolie
But as one nation with one destiny
Living in sweet peace and harmony

# *Addendum to* My GUYANA

After reading here about much hate
I have to stave off some racial spate
My Guyana includes Indian music and calypso
Of Ravi Shankar, Rafi, Mukesh and Sudar Popo
It's Indian music at an East Indian wedding
Where East Indians and blacks are dancing
And if you think Indians can dance really
To Indian or *tassa music* or hot *chatney*
You never see blacks wine down with *Nanee Wine*
Putting Indians to shame but all at that time is fine
It's a cultural thing from far away Africa?
Or the missing link that can heal Guyana?

My Guyana of course for sure is not one when
Some black bandits cut off the hair of our women
After they robbed them of all their life savings
After their usual molesting, raping and burnings
This is violent racial hatred and so very shameful
And one wonders if it's not Xenophobia so hateful
One must not forget what happened in Wismar man!
With Burnham's catastrophic genocidal *X-13plan*
Yet by other blacks it was never condemned
But they turn their faces or are just numbed

Or pretend not to notice these racial evils
Committed by their folks all be it devils

My Guyana is for who can stand up and be counted
Tell the molesters to stop or they would be dented
When wrongs are done to any other race
By those who talk nice before your face
When advantages are done to the mass
When eye-pass becomes real *rass-pass*
When we can go back to the days
Of yore of *live and let live* ways
When the villages were mixed with all peoples
By folks with churches with their own steeples
By both major races and all religion
Be it Krishna, Allah, Christ, or Zion
Living and working together *brother*
Which we used to call one another
Feeding from your pot and giving shelter
Even for the kids doing some sleepover
Not when night comes run for cover
From bullets coming like a shower
But as sure as the morning sun rises
After the pundits' analyses and surmises
My dreams one day will come true eventually
And finally we will be able to sleep peacefully
You can take that to the banks
And say nothing but thanks

# A GUYANESE XMAS

When I look back on my life
Before I had my loving wife
I remember from my childhood file
The good old Xmas Guyanese style
Long before Xmas December 25th would come
My village was astir be you foe or either chum
Folks preparing the home with drapes and blinds
And the Xmas cake by grinding fruits of all kinds

Whoever had the oven firing it up with care
As friends and neighbours go over to share
Before December 25th with the sweet aroma
Every mother waiting in line up with her quota
With buckets of mixed cakes ready
That's where would be the activity
With the women gossiping
And kids and pets frolicking
A fair-like atmosphere is taken on
With happy banter by everyone
And setting the cool ginger beer
Was done by an elder with care

What a blessed country with some of the best fruits
Maybe it's the silt of the rivers making good roots
Most Guyanese have very good lungs
Is it because of the sandy fine dungs
Guyanese girls have the sweetest lips
Is it because of the ripe juicy genips
We don't get cancer and have strong teeth
Is it because of the sugar cane or laba meat

No fruit can be compared with the sapodilla
Star-apple, Buxton spice mango or the cowa
Don't get me started on ground provisions bhaya!
The eddoes, tanias, the bell yams and the cassava
All boiled with coconut milk and hassar and some bhagee
And you have a delicious meal for the gods called metagee

A Guyanese Christmas is unique for sure
Can never be understood by a NA culture
Of hamburger, hotdogs and some spaghetti
As I eating my dholl puri and mutton curry
Our six peoples each have a tasty dish
Some still enjoy foo foo and salt fish
And from waterside to the sand reef
Our Muslim brothers prefer their beef
And from Corentyne or Buxton
The Hindus mostly eat mutton
During this time the air is filled with jukeboxes
To describe it there aren't any modern phrases
Blasting of melodious Indian songs and chatney
From a people known for their fine hospitality

There is no good or proper real Christmas over here
Without a piece of fruitcake and a glass of ginger beer
Here, there is so much stupid eye pass
Some don't want you to say **Merry Xmas**
The faiths are so afraid to connect
Saying you're not politically correct
Keep your fake Xmas tree and darn snow
Shoveling your snow only makes me blow
One day! one day! I hope in my lifetime alas!
Yes! I still can have my old Guyanese Xmas

# THE LOADED DUNGS TREE
### (The Dead Donkey)

It seemed to me as a young boy
Like our dungs tree was always bearing
As I pulled my jug-bull-cart toy
Steering my *jhuwat* nearby but looking
None would've anything to do with it at all
Its sharp pimples were a big problem
But we eyed the ripened dungs about to fall
Waiting for our turn to pick them

Just behind the house it stood
Forever dungs-loaded and sprawling
The sandy fruits tasted so good!
Which we picked with little goading
My father tied his beast under the tree usually
One day it decided to be very stubborn
He'd flogged the daylights out of the donkey
We found it dead the very next morn

To pick the fruits we got so scary
So as not to let the good fruits go wasted
Because of the poor dead donkey
And I still remember how the fruits tasted

Seer would fill up her big basket
From the big *full a plimpla* laden juicy dungs tree
She sold them at the local market
We stopped eating them because of the dead donkey

# MY BLOOD IS IN YOUR SUGAR

Sweet sweet sugar
Less than a dollar
A whole pound
From the ground
Left by slaves
Poor knaves
Their sweat and tears
For all dem lang years
Where my forefathers cut cane
Risking licks mek he go insane
Their blood so gud
In the black raw mud
With many callused barefeet
To mek something so sweet
Loading punt
As they grunt
Pulling heavy punt
Munth afta munth
Years after years
For five long years
With the bakrah like a leech
Until we indentureship reach
As you sit and chataay
Sucking at your latte
Asking for your double double

Not realizing the damn trouble
It took to bring that shuga
Cubes from sunny Guiana
To your comfortable table
Hey man! It's no stupid fable
Today you tek it for granted
Done by slaves who wanted
To run away far from the plantation
For you can't tender yuh resignation
As Massa munch on tea and cake
When they do call for a break
Time to wash off all the grime
For hunger was never a crime
Stuff down me stale roti
With some left ova curry
Wash it down with black middle-walk wata
Feeling so hot feel I can swim back to India
Avoiding the eyes of the **lead-hand**
He's nothing more than a brigand
For although he is one of us
He's a man you cannot trus
He will sell you down the riva
Just to please his damn Massa
Back to work Oh god!
Tek me now Oh Laad!

The sun is going down once more
And I know I'll be back for sure
I got no way else to go
I go as the hardship flo

Where's all de promises what a life
Maybe one day I'll find a good wife
These bastards told us about
As they smile and they shout
Nice country, new lives! nice Guiana!
Betta me bin stay me fat ass in India
Than come to this hell hole
Guh get lots a full rice bowl
But I see a bahin smile this afternoon
I hope she don't think I'm a buffoon
Only her sweet smile keeping me alive
That's what I'm living for all the while
One day one day we gun hook up
Maybe at the end of this crop
And we gun build a lil benab
If only the Massa won't rab
Me, give me my promised land
But I hope to God he understand
Then me and me sweet bahin
Guh marry and raise some kin
And hope one day one day
When dis damn denturship end
And when I hope I can still bend
We can leave this hell hole Guyana
And go back home to Mother India

# REMEMBER WISMAR

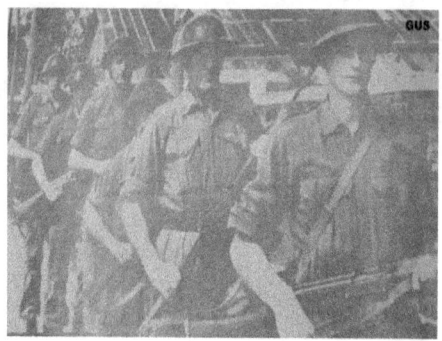

It was a dark and red-lettered night
They swept down on peaceful Wismar
Leaving a people in a miserable plight
Leaving each with an indelible scar

The mastermind was the infamous Chippy
Whose ambition was to kill every man
Woman and child in that peaceful community
By carrying out the evil X-13 Plan

They swept viciously on doves like hawks
With blazing guns and set bayonets
Annihilating all that walks and all that talks
Sparing none with their racial bullets

Not even the sleeping babies escaped
Or the pregnant women and mothers
Even the young and aged were raped
Even the children and little sisters

And as if that was not enough for these animals
All the innocent females were defiled
And many were crippled as in historical annals
Of wars of the barbarous and the wild

After they butchered the inhabitants
They did their looting and burning
Pillaging the shops and restaurants
And swiftly left Wismar a-smoking

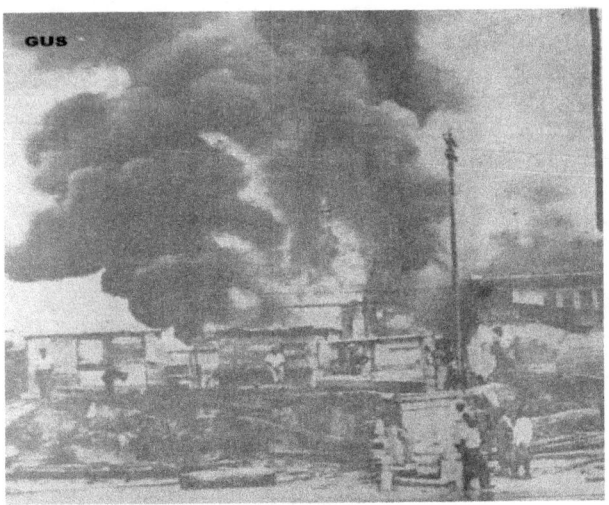

Yes! they left the city ablaze
And the waters red with blood
This was only the first phase
Leaving body parts in the mud

Death was welcomed by those in excruciating pain
As the waters of the Demerara carry the chill
Many committed suicides and many became insane
And their plight is always remembered still

 And on a very still or clear day one can hear
The cries of babies and women's groans from afar
The wailing wenches and women in agony and fear
Amidst the flow and ebb of the waters of Wismar.

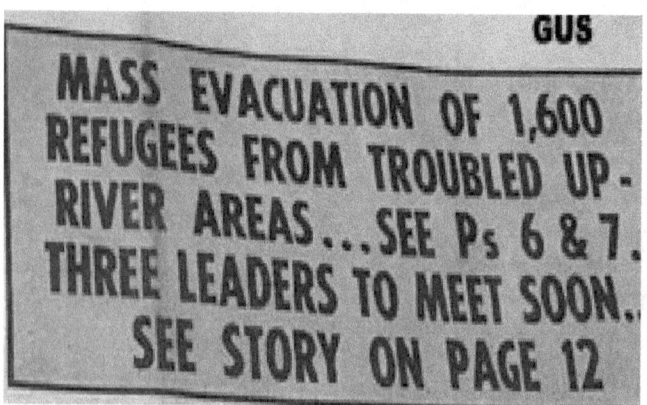

# THE NON PARIEL UPRISING

Our visitors to Guyana from other places
Were all treated with respect in all cases
This is a tradition engrained in our genes
Not to bludgeon them with our peens
Although some claim to be inventive
Our visitors were so very insensitive
Yet our slave masters treated us very harshly
Although we were loyal with good husbandry
Enslaved our men reducing them to mendicants
Handing out pittances showing poor judgements
Dehumanizing our women with sheer disrespect
Callously neglecting complaints left unchecked
A high percentage of them were educated peoples
Yet they were all mal-treated worst than weevils
And many also had a great deal of oral learning
Despite their humbling and lead-hands' bashing
Many were also gifted with artistic and technical skills
They left India to come to save the *bakrahs*' sugar-mills
A large number of Indian *Sepoys* (soldiers) among them
Unlike the white comrades-in-arms they had no problem
They were not drawn from the dregs of society

They were members of a very respected army [8]
Not taking the Queen's shilling as a last resort
But for the bakrahs to give adequate support
Always well dressed in uniforms or in tunics
Whether they were Hindus, Muslims or Sikhs
They regarded their calling as warriors
And served as the bakrahs' protectors
Sepoys *(soldiers)* of the British Indian Army
Had faith in Hinduism, Islam and Christianity
Several were also men of high learning
Many were literate with good breeding
Versed in Latin, Religious Studies and Astrology
Also Mathematics, Commerce and Astronomy
Lord Louis Mountbatten who once had visited Guyana
Thought the coolies were magnificent men from India
Their tall figures, deep broad chests, and molded limbs
Showed as if they spent all their spare time in the gyms

Interfere with a mother's kid, see how she would respond
Interfere with a man's wife you can't even hide in a pond
That's what caused this whole morbid sordid affair
For women living in the logies was like a nightmare
The logies offered very little or no privacy
Abduction of women was done very easily

------

[8] *The term sepoy or sipāhi is derived from the Persian word "sipāh" meaning "infantry soldier" in the Mughal Empire. The term sepoy came into use in the forces of the British East India Company in the eighteenth century, where it was one of many, such as peons, gentoos, mestees and topassess used for various categories of native soldiers. Initially it referred to Hindu or Muslim soldiers without regular uniform or discipline.*

This was mostly done by overseers and managers
And yes also from some community members
Who would stoop to any level they can find
And most  times it was  for cash or for kind
Firstly, the Harry Garnett the Manager of the sugar estate
Went to **Gerad Van Nooten** who raped Jamni as a bedmate
Van Nooten and friends were habitual violators
Of our immigrant women, girls and daughters
Mr. Garnett should have placed Van Nooten on an anthill
When he said he was keeping Jamni of her own free will
Of course Van Nooten's claim by Jamni was denied
She struck him in his face then he started to backslide
With heavy steel **berwas** (*bangles)* she wore on her wrist
She scratched his face as he attempted she tried to resist
Van Nooten released her and she ran towards her **lojie**
A group of armed men including her husband, Jangli
Demanded the manager brought to justice
Only to be told their protest had no basis
Despite all the lies told by managers to get their fill
Few females lived with them on their own freewill
To give themselves to the management officials
Too scared of retaliation fighting their own battles
They staunchly hold on to their cultural traditions
And offered resistance to males with evil intentions
Biased and headstrong Capt.De Rinzy went into action
Disorder ensued, angry workers heedless of protection
As he unwisely conspired not even to enquire
Instead he ordered his militia squad to open fire

After the shelling settled with the bullets and buck shot
Jangli and one worker were shot and killed on the spot
Three others died and 59 were injured with buck shot fire
Because the manager wanted to fulfill his sexual desire.

# BECHU

In 1894 Bechu came
Long before Ayube Eden
Or Jagan entered the game
This fearless fighter
A *kurmi* by caste
From across the calla pani
From Calcutta
Bound for Enmore
Sugar Plantation
As a domestic servant
To make his mark

He was 36 and smart
Thanks to a white missionary
Bechu got educated
A man of courage
Braver than Koffy or Acara
The likes you've never seen
In those harsh times
When the good dies

He knew the indentured system
He stood up and was counted

But with a silent rage
And had Ram on his side
He knew the words
He wrote letters
Was the only man
To fight the darkness
Who gave a memorandum
To the Royal W. I. Commission

He condemned
The indentured system
Attacked their long cruel hours
By estate drivers
Ungodly wage reductions
A wage of 25 cents a day
He revealed the horrors
Oh the bully estate *sardars*
Using *task work* to coerce workers
Using henchmen
To threaten and silence
Those who complained
He stressed the willful neglect
Of the immigration department
Failing to protect
The wretched Indians

And then this fearless
Kurmi did the unbelievable
Armed with only the holy Gita
He denounced in no uncertain terms

The immoral sexual relations
Between the mighty estate personnel
And helpless Indian women
He exposed the white overseers
Who kept Indian women
On the side
On several estates
As if running brothels
He exposed the case
Of *Lello* and the Punjabi
He showed how such
Immoral behaviour
Produced discontent
Poor production
And sheer resentment

He exposed them
As in the case
Of the Non Pariel riots
Stemmed from the affair
Of a married woman
And an evil estate manager
He accused the demonic
Manager *Frederick Bascom*
Of Plantation Cove & John
Of causing the death
Of poor sick *Bhagri*
Discharged from hospital
While he was still sick

Then to silence Bechu
They charged him with libel
Tried him twice
Threatened to deport him
Back to Mother India
Then they surreptously
Quietly left him alone
Not wanting to spark
Another labour riot

Every time someone
Came to champion the cause
Of the wretched Indians
They were silenced
Or paid a heavy price
For their bravery
And their courage
Like heroic Bechu
But what made them winners
They had a strong dharma
And the guiding hand of Ram
Who sent heroes like Eden
The indomitable Jagan
And the mighty Bechu.
To champion their cause.

**NB.** *If Bechu was related to Sarojini Naidu's father, Aghoranath Chattopadhyay, then Bechu's family name would have been Chattopadhyay. Bechu came on the Ship Sheila to British Guiana in 1894 as Immigrant No. 68157 and indentured to Enmore at the Non Pariel estate. Bechu might have died somewhere on the west coast of Demerara as he was a very sick person.*

# CHILDREN OF THE JAHAJIS

They made homes in Guyana, Trinidad, Jamaica
Martinique, even Venezuela and tiny Grenada
St.Vincent, St. Lucia, Honduras, Guadeloupe
French Cayenne and also in the Dutch group

After five years they were freed from their **massahs**
Many were lured with false promises by **harkatiyas**
With free passages back to Mother India
Of easy jobs in the islands and Guyana

Their hopes and aspirations were shattered
From estate owners as they were scattered
By the treatment and racial molestations
On the cocoa, corn and sugar plantations

Living in long logies of mud and wattle
The **massahs** handled them like cattle
And they met worse humiliating fates
When they had to face the magistrates

His rights were always met with denial
He was charged and dubbed a criminal
**Breaching** the indentureship contract
For the massahs were mean and exact

The reward for saving the English plantation
When the Negro slaves got their emancipation
Was turning them oppressed into slavery
To save the bakrah's dilapidated economy

Negroes made life very uneasy
Calling them **Babu** and *coolie*
They ridiculed and molested them
On top of all their other problem

They mocked their Hindu religion
Called them pagans treated them as foes
Molesting the youths were common
So was the ridiculous abuse by Negroes

The Indians suffered traumatic attacks
They couldn't live in peace and couldn't win
East Indians were forced to marry blacks
**Dougala** meant straighter hair and fairer skin

In many islands they lost their names and religion
And they were completely integrated
Only then they were more tolerated as kith and kin
And then they were readily accepted

No one was even in the Fast Indians' niche
The plantation owners had the law on their side
For the magistrates were owned by the rich
And Indian field-workers were in for a long ride

The Negro later became a black Whiteman completely
They almost lost their religion and were culture dead
Were bent on forcing the Indians into their society
Like them, only to become **brown white men** instead

Now the Indians are the wealthiest in the Caribbean
In Guyana, Trinidad and Suriname they are the majority
The **Coolie Baboos** are educated, self-made and keen
And owned most of the businesses, land and property

Like the little train which says it can
Was the indomitable Cheddi Jagan
They raised very learned men and not lagabagoos
Like the famous Shridat Ramphal and the Luckhoos

In our Law, men were decent and not mean
Ramsahoye and  Mohamed Shahabudeen
In Education they were men of higher mind
Birbalsingh, Ravi Dev and Rupert Roopnarine

For the suffering from the Socratic oath's basin
Dr. Mootoo and Dr. Balwant Singh in medicine
In our religious affairs we were honoured above all
With Bisnauth, Pt. Daman Persaud and Mulavi Ali

In Business Toolsie Persaud, Abdool Gafoor and  Beharry
Yesu Persaud, Kayman Sankar, the Kissoons, and Mazaharally
All were stalwarts in their respective fields doing their own thing
The military gave us Balram Raghubir and Major General  Singh

Moses Dwarka was our champion in athletics
In track and field he thrashed them with licks
Shakira Baksh was our beauty ambassador
Not forgetting our beautiful Nalini Monasar

Dr. Rovin Deodat and Ricky Singh our media best
J.W. Chinapen and David Dabydin passed the test
Rajkumari Singh spearheading our Arts and Culture
Devindra Pooran and Pita Pyaree, our new future

With Lakshmi Kallicharran and Paranand Sukhu
Nadira Shaw, Pandit Gossai and Mohan Nandu
And Gora Singh some of the best who broke through
Also Sammy Baksh, and Gobin Ram just to name a few

These pioneers who came from Mother India
Are the East Indians today with a proud dharma
That's still practiced with vigor and zest
For they had the stamina to come West

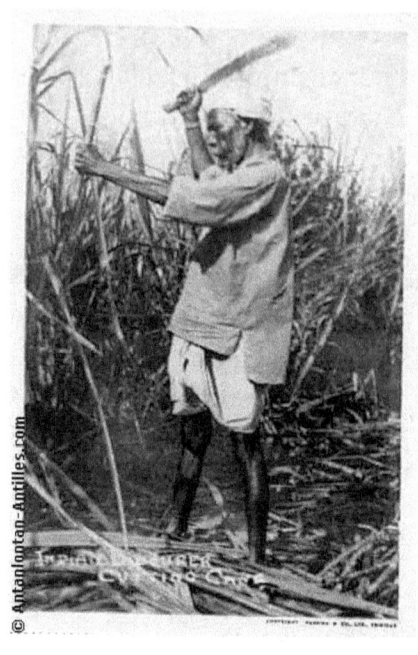

# THE CANE-CUTTER

Fo-day manin-cack a crow
And he know he gat to go
And all he gat is he sharp twenty-two
And he food-carrier so shiny and new

Today is had wok this whole munth
Today we gat to full all dem punt
At break-time me tek a lil smoke
And Kadwah guh crak a lil joke

And then the dam lead-han'
Playing lek some white man
Sometimes behave like a real jerk
Come and chase us back to work

Buddy-by how me bones ah ache Oh Gad!
If when Haray Ram tek me now, me glad
Only Ram keep me going as I chant me bhajan
Today, I hope me wife cook hassar and sigan

The cane-cutter tek his roti from he carrier-dish
He is thinking of his last daughter's only wish
To save ebry las cent of he salary
To pay for her damn big dowry

Po gyal na know fuh wat in store
But agat to let me baby go fuh sure
Oh Gad! Now I can hardly bend
When does all dis hadship end?

The cane cutter goes home at sunset
Gat to hurry so he wifey don't fret
Still gat sum tumatee to plant
So tired no matta how he cant

Fatnight coming and its pay day
Gat to tek a lil finey this Friday
Shoot some crap wid Kak, Bud and Lulluby
And Pum-pak to dance wen he get lil groggy

Betta read yuh book get some larning
You can't last wid this cane cutting
You cut, fetch and full punt in de sun or rain
Come Munday and  it's back to cutting cane

Pickney ah tell yuh dis life is haad
Dis is nat cricket or playing cyad
Yuh wuk till yuh get haad calluses all ova
And de bakrah neva say thanks, son-of-a

The cane-cutter is one of those dying breed
These pioneers've fused the Guyanese seed
Metal intact, they raked and did scrape
And eventually changed the landscape

# DOWN BY THE SEASIDE

Some folks call it the waterside
I yearned to go down the seaside
To watch out for the big long ships
As they plunge and take their dips
I'd go into the water as far as to my waist
And let the far flung sprays slap my face
I lie on the gray sandy beach
A Budwiser within my reach
Watching an ugly dark carrion badger
Thinking I am ready for his next dinner
Gone are the mangroves and crab grass
Replaced with bungalows and *eye pass*
The once pure beach by the seaside
Polluted by junk from their last ride
The shores have now become real eyesores
The *four-eyes* hardly come near the shores
Once I remembered how some friends and I
By the Koker[9] from the rains trying to defy
As we all took shelter by the **Big Saline**
Uncle Flood came along lanky and lean
Drenched with full quake and cast-a-net
**'Wanna a fish bhys**?' We said, '**You bet'**
We had built a fire to keep us warm
The wind was becoming a windstorm

---

[9] ***Koker is a Dutch work for Sluice***

We roasted a fresh catfish as the rains fell
The fire burnt out the rank and the smell
And that catfish tasted so darn delicious
Some would say that would be tasteless

And as I lazily lie I get a lot of memorable hints
Maybe Columbus passed here leaving footprints
On that same beach only yesteryear
We gamboled there without any fear
Curry and I chased the plover birds to be curried
Simon and Hardat flipped a long wire at high speed
We collected every fluttering juicy plover
Chasing those which are running for cover
On the same beach by the swamplands
We pulled out crabs with our bare hands
Not too far off we caught *carey-carey*[10]
With a decoy bird using *gama-cherry*[11]
Placed on some dense *belly-ache* trees
As we waited nearby in the cool breeze

Then I hear music so loud and rude
Shattering and disrupt my quietude
Some ragamuffins apparently gone astray
Looking for easy pickings on which to prey

---

[10] *A smaller version of the parrot*

[11] *Gama-cherry is a fig-like fruit which yields a good paste, locally
used for pasting kites.*

Back to civilization after that very long stroll
Down the Middle dam passing by **North Pole**
Going to the sea-shore feeling the sweet breeze
Yes Bush Lot is the darn best village in Berbice
When I went back to Bush Lot a few years ago
My friends have left or passed away a big blow
I'm very sad for Bush Lot has that special space
For me it's sweet home, yea! it's a special place!

---

9 *A local watering hole or rumshop at Bush Lot, W C Berbice, Guyana*

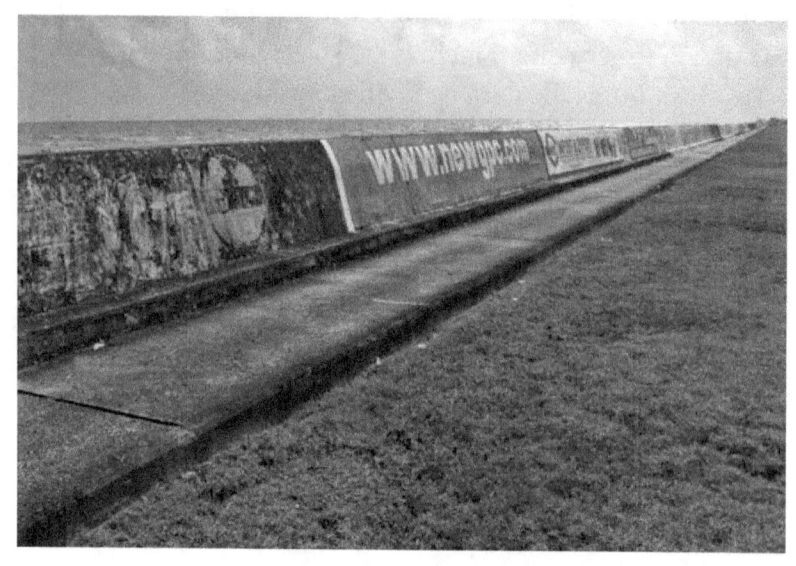

# THE SEA WALL

Always blasting the old coastland
From Point Playa to Springland
Daily taking the beating and all
Was and is the good old Sea Wall
Firstly built by the good old Dutch
And now have some other's touch
Like Don Quixote she clasped the waves
Reminiscent of Guyana Arawak's braves
With dirt and concrete so reinforced
Battling the Atlantic Ocean's course
Eight feet below sea level still

As the foaming froth try to fill
The land with her muddy salt sea water
Standing her ground and getting stronger
Over spill sucked up by waiting crab-grass
As the sea wall looks upon this as **eye-pass**
And the waters shyly ebbs away
Only to be returned another day
The old man watching the brackish waters
Heedless of the local bat and ball cricketers
Waiting  for the right time and tide
To throw his cast-a-net far and wide
As a gull flitters nearby as an imp
For the discarded fish or shrimp
And life goes on as farmers forge ahead
Thinking of their crops and homestead
Not knowing how much pressure it'd take
Or when and where the sea-wall could break

The sea-wall is alive as day is nearly closing
Some come for walks others at their choosing
Lovers holding hands and watch the sunset
True and even taboo unions try to forget
What will befall them with their confessions
For then inter-marriage could cause fractions
Partly the sea-wall is covered with graffiti
As trustful hearts keep it out of boundary
The wall can tell of broken hearts and tears
Of peers and fears which fell on deaf ears
And as you follow the sea-wall to the city
You see lovers smooching in many an alley

They are on bicycles or just standing
Looking into one another's eyes talking
As the waters lash the sea-wall with sprays
Likewise hearts and desires are in a blaze
Looking across the sea each with  dreams
For life abroad hatching plots or schemes
Concentrating on emotions so fervent
Oblivious of all in that environment

# CHAPTER III

# POLYTRICKS & POLITICS

1. **PEACE & WAR**
2. **TORTURE & REVENGE ( BULLYING)**
3. **MANKIND IS NOT VERY KIND**
4. **TO WAR OR NOT TO WAR**
5. **KILLERS IN OUR MIDST**
6. **FAKE IT TO MAKE IT**
7. **THE SINS OF THEIR FATHERS**
8. **THE DARK ENGLISH HEART**

**9.**

# PEACE AND WAR

Our very real troubles in this life
Was because of a war or a peace
Our society is built on confusion
Whenever there's peace in one part
War will break out in another region
And the people are so brainwashed
The truth they never can ever see
They've been succumbed to strife
Of men trying to mark their crease
And ended up in mass delusion
Not putting the horse before the cart
Too dedicated to their party's legion
Preferring to be mentally thrashed
By man's sheer evil hypocrisy

We haven't learnt from history
Repeating the same, same old mistakes
Like the Arabs and the Jews
From since the times of Goshen
They are still at it in the Middle East
Haven't learnt anything from the Irish
The Tamil Tigers of the same school
The Indian and Pakistani story
Cause you can't eat and have your cakes
Then go and pray in your pews
As they are doing now in Iran
Where war is their own loving beast
Learnt from their teachers the British
Who taught them to divide and rule

# TORTURE AND REVENGE
## *(BULLYING)*

What manner of man
Cause he has power can
Perform tortures and then kill
Carrying out his master's will
Cutting off hands and feet
All they claim just to defeat
When you take a stance
By democratic resistance
Using an iron rod with a condom
Picking out *kaffirs* at their random
Inserting it in women's private parts
Just as well tearing out their hearts
All the atrocities they breached
After leader Mandela preached
And bringing it all in the open
This was no parroting token
By his truth and Amnesty Commission
As all those culprits beg for Salvation
Their answer was they did it patriotically
So that the white folks can sleep safely
For the love of the fatherland
That I can never understand

# MANKIND IS NOT VERY KIND

Some of our nation's leaders've set a bad example
As they abuse, exploit, mowed down and trample
The very good people who put them in power
Yet when rebuked or condemned they shower
Them with long bullets as in the ***Arab Spring***
Where the wrath of the people is still ringing
From Yemen to Morocco
The Arabs have gone loco
Finally coming to their senses
They've broken down defenses
Putting an end to autocracy
Replacing it with democracy
***Be careful of what you wish for!*** they say
Ensure you're not caught in a political estray
In the West mankind is very unkind too
At times biting more than he can chew
Sometimes he is too proud to admit he's wrong
Instead of waving and singing his patriotic song
As in the case of Uncle Sam
Camouflaged as a big scam
The most powerful country in the world
Running around with it's flags unfurled
As millions of folks are without medicare
As the two parties jostle for votes in fear

Here the rich can get away with murder
Paving their way with a sly good lawyer
Some are caught quickly in quagmire
Plying their trade as a suicide bomber
Many innocent folk suffers and get hurt
As innocent by-standers lose their shirt
Some unkind men pillage the earth
Extracting and weakening its girth
From the oil, coal and iron mines
Aggravating so many fault lines
Then there are the vultures
Who disregard all cultures
They are below man's feces
Killing endangered species
They prey upon the weak and poor
Dispensing all their hard drugs to them
Luring them into an addiction problem
Just for the green backs
Using AK-47 in attacks
And so it goes even when caught
It always turned out to be naught
For the Drug-lords sold their souls
They know all the law's loopholes
Then they are the real hypocrites who really pray
They're the ones who go to church every Sunday
Their sole evil intention all hell-bent
Was to make Barak a one term President
And then go to the big White House arena
Debating issues to benefit the taxpayer
Using filibustering as their con

Eventually nothing is being done
Mankind has become very cruel
Behaving worst than a darn fool
Where men abuse women and children
Done solely by machismo egotistic men
Single mothers become the breadwinners
The grand-parents become the care-takers
And children without parents to love
Look for it in all places but not *Above*
Many fall in cracks by the wayside
Then they are in for a long hard ride
Mankind who used to be your brother
Sadly today they're killing one another
And there is fundamentally very absent
Respect for each of the commandment
We really have to back to the basics
Discard our hypocrisy and tricks
Respect the laws of nature
Do not be so darn cocksure
Stop texting learn to talk to one another
And returning being our brother's keeper

# TO WAR OR NOT TO WAR

War was made by man everyday
To thin the population some say
From times immemorial
To our present times social
It's been going on and on in every land
Mr. Mighty always have the upper hand

Before times of Mahendro Daro or Harripa
Before India was ruled by the Mahabharta
By armies of atomic power and rage
It's still happening in this modern age
No more spears and camels are used
Now its stealth bombers so very fused

The English had their heyday once
They sent the Armadas in defence
To pillage and plunder for the royal sake
Headed by Hawkins and Francis Drake
Yesterday Bush used Chiney and it's done
And in no time a war is sometimes won

How many more youths have to die and
To defend the Fatherland and Motherland
Vietnam took so many yet they've lost
Fighting an enemy at a tremendous cost

In the end a whole country was forsaken
Leveling its flora and 58,000 were taken

Israel sandwiched between her enemy's lap
Who still want to wipe her off the global map
Fighting a losing war backed by her kith and kin
Who knows fully well they can never ever win
Everyday youths die on both sides of the borders
By men in high towered barriers giving the orders

First we used wars to manipulate
Today they're used to amputate
Mind control in nothing new
It was used by the Mayans too
Technology has gone so far on the net
Don't know what to fathom further yet

War has taken so many lives of dead wounded and foes
More than any natural disaster be it quakes or tornadoes
And yet still men who know better continue to rattle
Create mischief and provoke other nations to battle
War has become an incurable disease
When would we ever live in peace!

# KILLERS IN OUR MIDST[12]

The good dies and the sick goes to prison
As drug lords and war-lords vie for terrain
The Merchants of Bay street smirk
Dry dust settles and hurt feelings subside
It's life in a zoo of the 21st century

Getting wiser to battle new viruses
Yet ruthlessly emptying the rain forests
Butchering and dissecting good mother earth
For precious minerals and evil believers
As non-believers pollute our blue planet

What have we become without our humanity
When we lie and die for the almighty dollar
Stifling the truth for our selfish ambition
Using the flag or religion as a crutch
And grasping nothing from history

The truth, feelings, pride are still alive
And the good will always
For after deleting the violence and vices
Deep down man is a good person
When he can forgive and be charitable

---

[12] *This poem won the November 2003 Editor's Choice Award for Outstanding Achievement in Poetry presented by the International Library of Poetry /Poetry .com*

# FAKE IT TO MAKE IT

Have you ever seen how
Some even fat as a cow
Are so happy and go lucky
Appearing to be so crazy
But don't care what you think
Even if they're the missing link
And what you do they don't care a shit
They know they've to fake it to make it

You may think this is nonsense
And these people are very dense
Little do you know Mac
They are on the right track
Where they got it from I do not know
I know when I really see them glow
It cannot be that entire bad look as the alternative
Better to be with them than those who are negative

You have to believe and understan'
That every living person every man
Is connected to one another
We are all like one brother!
What ever we do affects the other person
And the wrongs we do make it worsen
The elements join us together spiritually
We've live as one or die individually

# THE SINS OF THEIR FATHERS

If folks do really believe in charity
Which preaches, ***thou shalt not kill***
Then according to the laws of divinity
If you kill your life just becomes nil

And I think that would mean
The owners of slave plantations
Changed what might have been
Sinning the 3<sup>rd</sup> and 4<sup>th</sup> generations

If we go back not long ago to the slave trade
Fostered and mastered by the Bakrah
Who wanted to stamp all things ***English made***
By the sweat and blood of cheap labour

If we go way back a bit further back
And look at the history of the French disasters
And review the Fr. Republic attack
Who cold-bloodedly guillotined their Fr. masters

The Spanish too also had their heyday
Forcing the Indians to be slaves with their whip
Murdering millions to get their own way
As their wives sip tea and kids play and skip

Recently the Germans did their share
They gassed millions of their own Jews
As other Europeans showed no care
Today they're getting what they chose

They say rule Britannia - ***Britannia rule the waves***
They thought their pride made them invincible
When they were ruling the peasants and the slaves
After losing their colonies now they're so humble

Today and then these the same people
Went religiously to church every Sunday
Treating their slaves worse than weevil
Whipping and working in every darn way

If there's a God then the prophecy
Being fulfilled today is very right
The result is a cancerous society
And no cures so far not in sight

And their children's children's children
For their fathers' sins would be punished
The off springs now men and women
Living a culture where life is diminished

Maybe that is why cancer is so common
All over the world mostly to Caucasians
A disease so far, which so far has won
And hardly affect Asians and Africans

If you believe in this dogma
Then surely the Bible is not wrong
Or else you think its karma
And wish to sing the Hindu song

Reincarnation throws light on this predicament
You become a lesser breed
Is aids and cancer being part of the punishment
The fruits of your evil seed

The North American is so darn obsessed
With making more and more money
That his soul has become dispossessed
And he is lost being very unhappy

If you believe there is a Zion
And sins fall on the third and fourth generation
Then this world of every Christian
Had to accept and seriously heed this stipulation

# THE DEEP DARK ENGLISH HEART

The nation in itself has been strangled by intrigue
Before they'd formed the UK, the first great league
The British dominated as far as could be seen
From Europe right down pass the Caribbean
To Asia Minor and down under
When they clap their thunder
Poor natives quake and obey
For only the English had a say
***Rule Britannia*** was their song
And they'd reigned very long
Anyone who resisted them
Got into serious problem
They knighted their robbers
Whom we called buccaneers
To them the British did no wrong
You're compelled to sing their song
To save their dilapidated sugar industry
Their righteous sole answer was slavery
This was one cause for their downfall
To feed the pot-bellied British and all

They did a lot of good which had stood the test
Their laws and education system were the best
Their snobbery and hypocritism and all
Left a deep dent in many an ex-colonial
They were so brainwashed with all the hypocrisy

Some still stuck up with their colonial mentality
What was once a shining lure
Is left today without a cure
The hidden heart of this once regal country's fates
Is a collection of very battered old housing estates
Red-light areas and inner-city ghetto
Singing *Rule Britannia* as their motto
Festered with crack houses living on the dole
Hoping for improvement with pole after pole
And a haven for all refugees and social exiles
Crooks, home grown terrorists and pedophiles
Really a place where the poor gather
Where colour or class doesn't matter
Snubbing or smirking at you in hat and cane as they pass
As you focus on the glass houses of the upper middle class

The rioters were leaving all things cheap
This was their harvest their time to reap
Why risk imprisonment if caught you query?
To them they had nothing to lose why worry
They had no jobs and no respectability
Nothing for them to pay off eventually
At the bottom of the barrel you can't scare
They'll face rubber bullets they had no fear
They were damaged goods all of them
The results of a fragile lopsided system
The plot thickens years ago into this predicament
The architect being the Conservative government
When **The Iron Lady** sold off public housing
Failing to replace it with zilch with nothing

Her **Big Bang** turned London into financial crisis
The result was huge bonuses, soaring house prices
Labour using welfare to save an economy already drowning
Doing his utmost to with its killing what Cameron is doing
So how do you feed of self esteem of your last grain
You riot and you even shame yourself you go insane

You steal junk that makes you feel posh
With your mates getting all that rush
You are filmed pretending to help a bleeding boy
But stealing from his back-pack is your real ploy
You do disgusting things giving blows
You break doors and smash windows
Ask why you doing this, you have no clue
As you take what you think belongs to you
For the poor has no one who is helpful
Especially when they turn out ungrateful
It is easier to report about who set the fire
But why they lit the fire in the first place sire?

# THE BLESSINGS OF THY FATHERS

Well aren't you better off than your homeland brothers
And better yet than your own fathers and your mothers
What blessings you may ask
Well that's not too hard a task
In India, Africa, China or southeast Asia
Even good old Europe or far off Guyana
Most of you have your own car, land or a fridge
A house with mown lawn with a wide frontage
And maybe some dollars in your bank account
And even a pony or horse in a stable to mount
For you're the products of a very proud heritage
And real honest pioneers who showed courage

Those who toiled today can show the results
In peace far from violence and nasty insults
When some tried to pray to Ram or Allah
Or to return to the Motherland of India
They were also struck dumb when they landed

Since then Motherlands aren't being demanded
Really! could this were where we yearned to go
The squalor, filth and poverty gave us a big blow
The caste system, and women's maltreatment
An ancient way of life so hideously indecent
Very shocking and disappointed we returned home
With thanks to our forefathers who left that dome

As many in America still complaining woefully
After 175 years about not given the opportunity
Still suffocating in food stamps and steep in welfare
Others are scraping and crawling to come over here
They're still blaming Caucasians for their freedom
As others risk deadly shark infested waters to come
And other immigrants just came over within decades
Doing the menial chores in farms, kitchens and maids
And they have risen above the standards of the natives
Who are still stewing over same old same old motives

Have they forgotten how their forefathers denied entry
To Sikhs [13],Jews [14],Haitians and folks from other ancestry?
Then the other motherland Africa still struggling
Blaming the west and others for their suffering
Her politicians and leaders forever in tribal warfare
Invade, defy, doing what they want without any care
As new leaders on the other side use machetes
Wiping out the opposition and also old cronies
Like toppled Somalia in warlordism and mass butchery
As little babies and women cry out like wailing banshee
Murder rampages of bewigged young men in Liberia
Ethnic genocide killings across the border in Rawanda

---

[13] *The Komagata Maru incident involved a Japanese, the steamship Komagata Maru, that sailed from Hong Kong to Shanghai, China; Yokohama, Japan; and then to Vancouver, British Columbia, Canada, in 1914, carrying 376 passengers from Punjab, India. Of them 20 were admitted to Canada, but the 356 other passengers were not allowed to land in Canada, and the ship was forced to return to India. The passengers consisted of 340 Sikhs, 24 Muslims, and 12 Hindus, all British subjects*

[14]*The MS St. Louis was a German ocean liner most notable for a single voyage in 1939, in which her captain, Gustav Schroder tried to find homes for 937 German Jewish refugees after they were denied entry to Cuba, the United States and Canada, until finally accepted to various countries of Europe. Historians have estimated that, after their return to Europe, approximately a quarter of the ship's passengers died in concentration camps*

Dumping their corpses into the Kagera River hard to find
Or into Lake Victoria, out of sight, better yet out of mind.

The USA running around in the name of democracy
Warring against anti this and that in every darn alley
Righting the wrongs or so they thought
Until they were ousted or were caught
Being branded the villain and infidel by some
Who never know the meaning of real freedom
But prolifcation of the west came from their motherland
Resulting in conquering every acre of Red Indian's land
Then came karma back to bite them elsewhere
Now left with warfare and steeped in welfare
At the same time preaching about their dying constitution
Sandwiched between the Second Amendment and Goshen

# CHAPTER IV

# THE NEXT CHAPTER

1.  CAN'T BUY BACK YOUR LIFE
2.  THE CONSUMER
3.  THE AMERICAN DREAM
4.  FROGS GONE
5.  SILENT DEADLY OCEANS
6.  JOHN GILBERT
7.  DUNCE
8.  YOU THINK YOU KNOW THEM
9.  WITHOUT SUFFERING THERE'S NO COMPASSION
10. ITS BETTER TO BE ALONE
11. THE HARD WAY IS THE ONLY WAY
12. WHAT HAPPENED TO THE FAMILY LIFE
13. WORDS MAKETH THE MAN

*By three methods we may learn wisdom: First, by reflection, which is noblest; Second, by imitation, which is easiest; and third by experience, which is the bitterest.*
<u>*Confucius (Kong Qiu)*</u>

# CAN'T BUY BACK YOUR LIFE

Some children demanding every cent
And their parents always so hell bent
In giving them every new toy they want
Or appease them into a fancy restaurant
They feel they can always buy them
But that never solves the problem
As Churchill once said
Before he was put to bed
Even if you appease an alligator
He'll eat you at last! much later

Some prefer to buy the love of their children
They'll do the same when they become men
They will buy the whole shop
And even work until they drop
But would never spend quality time
Or to read them their nursery rhyme
They would buy the latest gadget
Selling million dollars of widget
They go to church pray to the one above

But too busy with golf to show some love
They may work for a salary or wage
Too busy working for the mortgage
Never have time to see their kids in a play
But always have some lame excuses to say

And the kids really got hurt
They feel they are not worth
The love of either parents
And they do rebel hence
More work for the experts of the mind
Psychiatrists, physicians who unwind
These poor souls into category
All in the name of psychology
 They forget you can't buy back your life
You have one life to live as man and wife
Every day counts live it forget the roaming
The buck stops here dummy stop passing
It isn't to the government or school
It is in your very own backyard fool
Forget the daily highball and try to mend
For each day brings you near to your end

# THE CONSUMER

*When you lose the rhythm of the drumbeat of god, you are lost from the peace and rhythm of life.*
<u>*Cheyenne Proverb*</u>

If you believe in reincarnation
Then you may ask the lord
Not to return you as a consumer
Better for you to burn
Return to ashes or you may as well
Return as a mule or a bleddy jackass
Which is a beast of burden
For that's what a consumer is
I don't know who in tarnation
Arrived at such a dirty word
For the consumer is not any user
But the little man who try to earn
Eke out a living and can tell
About life when you belong to the mass
Being watched by the *Warden*
Who thinks only of business.

The sharks and sardines
Fat, lazy pompous cats
Who think it's the duty
Of the consumer to support

Them, their vices and heirs
Pleasures, pastimes and mistress
Thinking they have the darn right
To squeeze out that little extra
As done by juice machines
And later using them as doormats
Still ruminating from their booty
Oblivious of their purport
Because of contempt, greed or fears
Refusing to fight or mess
With Naders who have seen the light
In commercialized North Amcrica.

The rich cannot be called
Consumers, for their wealth
Has escalated them beyond that point
Where their feelings are numbed
Their attitudes are carefree
Their conscience is smothered
By luxuries and fat cheque-books
They have in other words, lost contact
With the consumer and walled
Themselves out by stealth
Turning a deaf ear rather than anoint
Another, but being succumbed
For they look but never see
Not wanting to be wooed
With hearts like that of the crooks
Becoming very mean and exact.

If one doesn't know where one's been
How can one know where one's going?
Born with oral silver spoons
With Cadillacs, sipping cola and rum
Whereas consumers are simple folks
Living close to the good earth
Embracing that mundane quality
Of respect for nature
Where they see and are not seen
And give without any preaching
Although they may be called buffoons
They will surely go to God's kingdom
They are caught up in every hoax
Because of their humble birth
Thriving for only a simple prosperity
And their honest stature.

He leaves his home at dawn
Picking his way among the traffic
By public transportation
With only a lunch pail
Loyalty and a few meager cents
In case of an emergency
And if not used
Will be returned to purchase
Ration not for his lawn
But for his family trying to lick
The politician's inflation
Like a tiger licking his tail

Hiding all the miserable dents
And all the loopholes he can see
Whilst he's amused
At their red tape and paper chase.

If there's no overtime when the last bell goes
He changes and mixes with the rat-race
Homeward bound by the subway
Even after a hard day's work
He may cook or minds the children
He waits for his wife afraid to watch TV
He decides and leisurely putters
Around the home and garden
At wife's arrival they'll discuss the throes
And worried lines on her faithful face
Retiring early for the day
Discussing the evils, which irk.
After some child guidance they'll send
The children to their homework lovingly
Mother and father sleepily mutters
Lapsing into a sweet dream of Eden.

The consumer's fear is not
Of criminals, offenders or muggers
No! He has a greater fear
The fear of going to the supermarket
Fear of the news on the radio
Television or newspapers
Blasting sad news of another increase
Of taxes, rent or food items

It appears men are caught
In a battle like warriors
Pitting one against the other to share
Their blunders when they blew it
Their false pride makes them show
A pretence to their supporters
As if trying to help to cease
The uprising of these problems.

His children go to school either separate
Or public like others
They are disciplined in body and mind
Taught at home to be careful
Considerate and punctual
Taught personal hygiene
Respect for other's property
Always be contented
Charity begins at home not by fate
Treat everyone as brothers
Show concern when one is in a bind
Family ties are strong and helpful
Coupled with this atmosphere of parental
Guidance, the home is warm and serene
Diminishing uncertainty
Causing a firm bond to be cemented.

He does not use a Mr. Coffee
But an ordinary kettle on the fire
No coffee-mate but milk, rich
With cream and grain sugar

Not with cubes
His sandwich for his  hungry lunch
Is always home-made
And he washes it down
Not with a martini
Which spoils good victuals, sire
But pure Adam's ale which
Is mixed with humorous banter
Not from tubes
Of TV, radio or highfalutin crunch
But of a past escapade
On his last trip to town.

His wife does the laundry
Some by hand so dampened
With soft or rain water
The clothes are neatly pressed
And 'though they may be old
They are very clean
Without wrinkles or static
And she never worries about the cling
He works in a factory
The workers never know what happened
To his around the collar
And many have confessed
To ill stories being told
About his seamed jeans
And though he may be a bit erratic
At work, he always goes home smiling.

He saves not for a vacation
But to buy his wife
A shoe due a year ago
Or his teenage daughter
Her first party dress
Or a toy for his four year old son
His last of five cheerful children
So tired from left-overs
Now showing signs of vexation
But being the pet of his life
Allowing him to be so
Unlike his loving mother
Showing signs of stress
He's from his father's mold
Who, it's just a matter of when
He'll be ready for covers.

Getting on with skin so corrugated
He is contented to go now
At least he has earned and gained
The respect of his generation
The love and warmth here
Will follow him forever
In the passing to the far great beyond
Leaving a long pleasant memory
Always religious, staid and dedicated
He'd say to him at his pow-wow
How he never feigned
They'll tell of his reputation

How he faced them without fear
For though poor; he was clever
He's steadfastly honest, never abscond
Or indulged in any skullduggery

With anti-pollution to clean the air
The government declared war
On the automobile industry
Who said ok, but we will dump
It on the consumer, likewise
Then they say energy is short, conserve
And now we have nuclear power
With another fatal accident
Like Harrisburg, we'll be in the atmosphere
Luckily we wouldn't have any scar
And any more scientific technology
The pinch at the gas pump
Recently was no surprise
When hydro said we have to reserve
Of electricity, no refund for the consumer
But hounded foe his last bent cent

Then came Science International
With kilometers instead of miles
Good-bye Fahrenheit, welcome Celsius
Hi! How are your kilopastels?
What's your stats in centimeters?
Wow! It sounds ridiculous
But the decision has been made
By a few misfits

With little benefit to us all
God knows what's next in their files
Creating so much confusion and fuss
Like rhetoric old bells
Now gas cost more in litres
Which is ludicrous
We need a gov't. of a different shade
Before we all lose our wits

The falsity of our system is very dumb
The government in the guise of economy
Brings in different types of program
Which doesn't help the consumer
One iota
But eventually the cost
After extensive research and waste
Would finally pass down to us
And as the federal provincial hum
The consumer waits in awed expectancy
Would it be another hi-way or dam
A catastrophe or a disaster
One extra
Billion less or the most
To find out if the beaver has a taste
Or if monkeys can travel in moon bus.

These boys have a financial lust
To find some fool-hardy scheme
Always in the name of research
Just to allow the elite

To fool around at cock-tail with funds
That can be spent to the benefit
Of the consumers, but no!
They prefer to waste millions
Bickering in the national circus
The politician's ultimate dream
Where some sit like dry birch
For the soup over there is so sweet
Thus making no waves because of bonds
Always smiling, ready and swift to shift
In the name of the party, to show
Fake loyalty even to the unions.

Do not think for one moment
That the consumer doesn't have dreams
Of places like Acapulco or Barbados
Of mortgage rates getting lower
So he might buy a home
Of owning a farm or cottage
Of giving up the costly TTC
Buying his own little automobile
But when he tries to cement
And thinks he is getting there, it seems
He's got to get ready for the gallows
To earn extra bread and butter
If he really that home
And not to lose his economic footage
Accepting life as he breathes heavily
Too numbed with tension to feel.

He is like the last
Of a large family of eight
Whose clothes are handed down
Whose shoes are always
One size extra or long
His shirts are knee length
With patches on his back and belly
His hat covers his eyes
Always expected to be mild
Follow unquestioningly straight
Without much of a sound
No matter what his father says
Even if it's wrong
Applying his spent strength
As he loyally pursues determined
To uphold the family ties.

Such is the plight of the consumer
As large corporations and government
Conjure to lure
With catch phrases and slogans
Especially at general elections
And as corporations try to bribe
In the guise of party contribution
And the fight goes on
Those outside want the power
Of course with the consumer's consent
To lure for sure

We suddenly become loyal Canadians
Who are asked to make this decision
Without looking at religion or tribe
With both sides building up the tension
Each trying to out con

The consumer wants to stay alive
Without fear of hikes
Of taxes and vital food prices
But the politicians smother
All of us with national unity
Sovereignty or referendum
In for four or five years
They always want another term
None cares if consumers die or thrive
Ride Volkswagens or bikes
If he can afford a whole bread or slices
No one has the time to bother
They're in for all their vanity
But the consumer must come
Sober without malice or tears
And again for another worm.

After the mud sliding is over
The consumer's caught in the middle
They draw up new schedules
Of long vacation and coffee breaks
Maybe all didn't go well
Because the modern rigger
Called the computer

Failed to compute correctly
The **has beens** run for cover
As the PM cries fuddle duddle
Those who breaks the rules
Are penalized for the consumer's sakes
For a by-election will tell
Who is really the winner
Maybe he'd be just another joker
To join the circus ceremoniously.

After spending millions in enumeration
The consumers wait
For the promised betterment
Which never comes like tomorrow
The vast sums could've been used
As an income-tax rebate
For fixing the attic or to buy ration
Or that longed for yearly delicacy.
During the last hectic election
They all promised to create
More jobs, now the consumers lament
They can't buy, beg or borrow
They feel ashamedly abused
Woe onto their tired fate
Must have election for the nation
All in the name of democracy.

He thinks they intentionally do not curb
All the ills of this society
For there'd be no need for government

Thus time is wasted on trivial trials
Useless inquiries and commissions
For information that can be obtained
From the man in the street
Preferring to keep many idle civil servants
Whose complacency can't be disturbed
Fomenting class and official barbarity
Disallowing the consumer to vent
His anger by red tape and denials
Flowered by fancy talk and omissions
Heedless of the level they attained
For the soup of the other side is so sweet
When you are rich and others are mendicants.

They now look down on them
As they make them wait in line
While they have breaks perpetually
Spending time gossiping in the washroom
'Cause of a hangover from inebriation
Like clock-watchers
Hiding in a closet manicuring nails
Or playing cards or dominoes
Perpetuated by a cultureless system
Saying if you don't wine or dine
You'd be singled out personally
Refusing to play ball in the coffee room
Or suffer the pangs of crude molestation
From body-snatchers
With tentacle prehensile tails
Potbellies, bowlegs and dirty toes.

Sometimes the females so defenseless
 Against their horny bosses
Are penalized for squealing
Which the corporation always hushes up
By pampering their executives
The pretty secretary either toe the line
Become an office plaything or quit
Depending on her financial status
Thus many women are overcome by stress
Refusing to have a few tosses
On the carpet by bluntly saying
No! And if the molestation doesn't stop
The last of the prerogatives
Is not to lament or whine
In such an environment you're a misfit
Getting another job is conscientious.

When the consumer doesn't extend
An invitation to a celebrity
It's not because he is a scrooge
It's because his home is bare
Without furniture or frills
And he is embarrassed
He thinks maybe you're too high
To come down on his clean floor
And would not want to bend
Sit with him and sip coffee
For you may be a staunch stooge
Without compassion and care

Without any trouble paying bills
Never been harassed
Greasing the hinges as you ply
Your hypocrisy that shows like a sore.

When he extends an invitation
To the high-brow
It's because he loves you as a person
Despite race, religion or creed
His humble hut is warm
He feels ten feet tall
As he tells of his past generation
For he is from a long line
Of those who survived by determination
Whose up-bringing allow
Respect to his peers as a person
Responding to the helpless in need
In the street or farm
And likewise to his call
Without asking for any consideration
For those were the days and 'twas fine.

He knows fully well
The consumers, his types
Are the back-bone of this country
His fore fathers are of the pioneer spirit
Who'd never say *die*
That's why he is of such
A moral fiber
That merchants or marines

Cannot show him hell
For he already had his swipes
With his foes back home in the infantry
Doing his time giving tat for tit
Which many others try
To follow for he was much
Of an untamed tiger
With watered eyes for those tainted scenes.

The consumers and others give wry smiles
When they discuss
The methods and skullduggery
You nurture with such hypocrisy
Telling and preaching how to save
Articles for recycling purposes
So much bull, yet we see daily
Their waste of material and energy
Lighting up government buildings for miles
Yet at poor us
They threaten and worry
With mannerisms and phrases so catchy
In advertisements, as they rant and rave
Dishing out ratings in large doses
From the radio and telly
In pretensive patriotic parrotry.

On recycling what happens to the proceeds
No one can say
Does it ever go to the consumer
Well ...er... bla...bla...bla...

Although the already taxed taxpayer
Has to separate, pack and parcel it
Shouldn't the profits be channeled
Back through some honest practical method
Like less tax, one of his dire needs
But nay I pray
The consumer is always the loser
Yet he is willing to give that extra
For he knows once again it's another
Foolhardy scheme geared to their credit
For which they'll try until they've pummeled
Out our juices and left us drying in the sod.

Once when merchants were men
With a conscience and a soul
The consumer was protected
Today he is scorned and pressurized
By officials who owe their very existence
To him and his high taxes
Which will get him
If he doesn't go voluntarily
With lean years numbering ten
Before he reaches his pension, his goal
'Though he willfully neglected
Burdened and financially circumcised
His role in society and in life is so immense
He stands tall and never waxes
One day he'll trim
The brigands to size eventually.

At last thanks to democracy
Free trade has been legislated
Despite national opposition
There were lots of promises and speeches
And only time will tell
But as always in the long run
When the problems start to unfold
The little men always feel the squeeze
Because of the politicians' fantasy
Too stubborn and constipated
To judge any situation
Being accustomed to fleece like leeches
Trying to fill a dry well
Eventually getting nothing done
Yet knowing he's been out sold
And will also pass like the breeze.

And aeons from now a visitor
From another galaxy
Finding what was once earth
Would be amazed at the marvel
Of the last of the consumers
For standing alone on a pedestal
Reciting time, weather and erosion
Perplexed aliens would discover
This symbol of peace and caliber
Showing its longevity
Pure serenity and mirth
Of graphic granite like marble

Masking all ills of the entrepreneurs
With a gigantic monument for all
Indelibly engraved with the inscription
***Here lies the TAXED TO DEATH Consumer***

# THE AMERICAN EMPIRE

Before we reached those financial quagmires
Long after the Indian or the Mogul empires
Headed by Genghis Khan
The fighting strongman
**Khorhee** Nero or Julius Caesar
Of the Roman Empire's Czar
The Nazi's Third Reich
They were and all alike
Stalin's or Lenin's communism
Of the Russian Empire's ism
The Napoleonic French mates
Or Elizabethan knighted pirates
The British Drake, Morgan or Walter Raleigh
The architects of the present day corporatocracy[1]
Who loved the queen and nearly did marry
Posing as hypocritical squires
Encouraged by all in their shires

The American Empire more dangerous, those bastards
And it is alive and sitting right in our own backyards

---

[1] *The corporatocracy the core of the Empire consists of the banks, corporations and governments. Their job is to expand and strengthen the system using hitmen and jackals. John Perkins "CONFESSIONS OF AN ECONOMIC HITMAN"*

It's called the American Empire
Using jackals and hitmen for hire
They also tried to build by fighting
With the usual plundering and warring
Within Korea and Vietnam
Which humbled Uncle Sam
And the stubborn Middle East
Now a fighting daring beast
Belittled and so shamed all the time
But they keep fighting in mud and slime
For war is big business no bother
And the enemy's fate didn't matter

Today men make trillions
And they steal millions
With such an abject poverty everywhere around us
The people lost hope how can they have any trus'
From every $100. worth of oil from South America
$3.00 goes to the people as in desperate Panama
Who don't have edible food or potable water
As myopic leaders got taken and then falter
How can men and women watch their kid
Knowing darn fully well what they did
Deliberately stifling third world growths
Siphoning away dollars meant for those
Who are starving in their wanton throes
Banking it away in foreign offshore
Thus avoiding paying taxes for sure
All for the sake of oil
Recoiling ready to foil

Anyone who protested against them ought
To be prepared to feel their diabolical wrath
Like how Jamie Roldos of Ecuador vanished
Like How Omar Torrijos of Panama perished
And about the natives what about them?
Answering, *starving is not their problem!*

Under the guise of philanthropic loaners
Leaving millions in TWC[1] as groaners
Sheltered under the IMF, USAID[2] BICI[3], cloak
And making democracy a sorry bloody joke
Be it a Prime Minister or a President
They will try until they make a dent
Through, blackmail, coerce or bribe
Finding the weakest link in the tribe
Because of oil, they'll reach their downfall
For their corruption has gone far too global
Be it loans, contracts, timber, gold, silver or tin
The wretched third world countries can never win.

---

1 *TWC=Third World Countries*

[2] *International Monetary Fund and United States Agency for International Development.*

[3] *Business International Commercial Institution*

# SILENT DEADLY SMOOTH OCEANS

Sometimes it's not so smooth
But very rude and very crude
Saying, ***pollute me and you'll see***?
And woe unto evil man's hypocrisy
I will send my tsunamis far up
From your coast to your hill top
Then next I'm calm with the children
And allow others to be able fishermen
Or deliver a message to a lover or girl
In a bottle the other side of the worl'

Like a mother my vast oceans feed
Mankind with her crustaceous need
Man has polluted Mother earth already
With their poison belching machinery
He's trying to do the same with ease
With the five oceans and many seas
His oil spills are all over
As innocent sea-life cower
Trying to float and lick
Off the black thick slick
He's destroys everything he gets
Turtles caught in old gill nets
Sharks got tangled in fishing gear
And man continues without any fear

Man has no pity and makes no apology
For killing off the weed eating manatee
He uses the oceans like a slump
For his own waste disposal dump
Bottles, cans the bloody plastic he can't keep
He let it go down, float and some go very deep

My rough waters as in Katrina
As you have seen in Louisiana
I showed man he can't escape from his sins
I did went berserk and raised his old coffins
They blamed it on Bush and Katrina
But it was the wrath of Mother Nature
So many time and time again
I show man he's going insane
Show respect to my land
Or you will join the band

A paradise to beachcombers who find their goods
Treasure of shells, stones, coins and hard woods
Which get preserved with the salt water
And become more expensive and better
Like the greenheart packed in blocks
Are used for our wharves and docks
In seawater they become more sturdy
And ideal for uses in places watery

You have deforested the trees to build your cities
As your expert pencil pushers show your frailties

The waters of the oceans and seas
Give life to boaters and shippers
Is Mother Nature's switch
A fail safe to prevent a hitch
Most or all the riverian farms rely on this
Without my tides there would be no bliss

Some of us feel we have the right
Do anything cause we have might
Like our present financial depression
Like we did with our global pollution
Now we have a punctured ozone layer
And now we suffer with bad weather
We belittle the melting of the ice-cap
And end up with a very bad severe rap

Now we have unforeseen flooding
Losing crops due to weather changing
Death and destruction of our vital flora
Eruption of new viruses and extinct fauna
We are in dire need
Or else we'll bleed
Better husbandry to value life's worth
And protecting life here on this earth
Or we'll go the same way without a word
Just like some frogs and the do do bird

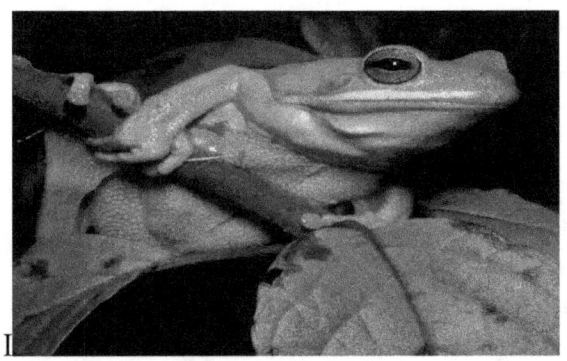

# FROGS GONE

We're here through the big bang
To some this is causing a pang
For this new generation
Believes in the evolution
But we have to stop if we can
If we want to save every man

However we came here
Forgetting we had to share
We did some things really crazy
Because of the need of money
Like wiping out the forests
That was a real super mess

The ozone layer so punctured
Man was never even deterred
Forgetting or playing forgetful

Each trying to get a handful
Blaming it on the economy
Just greed done stealthily

Sucking the earth of its cushions
As millions starve for rations
Extracting minerals, oil and its worth
Making giant holes in Mother Earth
Stacking it all the way into foreign banks
Too busy and carefree even to say thanks

We wiped out some species
Despite unwritten treaties
Of animals, snakes and some insects
As man bisects, dissects and infects
Stirring up dangerous viruses
Forgetting to cover our bases

Then on top of all that waste
To get the oil in so much haste
We had our share of oil-spills
Unheeded of whatever it kills
Damaging the fishes and birds
Disguising it with cheap words

Maybe if it's not too late
We need more than fate

We have seen the last of the **boreal toad**[a]
The **common-fire salamander**[b]
The **oophage sylvatica**[c], the **prismantis sp**[d]
And the **golden poison** frogs[e]

Smart man flooded the rivers with salmon
The salmon ate the tadpoles
And the frogs disappeared
Now smart man is trying
Deliberately forsake our real worth
Continue destroying Mother Earth

Don't turn your cheek and leave it to them
We all aided in destroying the ecosystem
We've to suffer the ecological consequences
For we've lost most of our basic defenses
What is at stake is our human welfare
Globally we all have to show we care

So we will have a new chorus
After some of us fight and cuss

---

[a] *Anaxyrus (Bufo) boreas* grows up to 5 inches declining

[b] *Salamandra salamandra* grows up to 10 inches, declining

[c] At Pontificia Universidad Catolica del Ecuador up to 1.5inches long and declining.

[d] At Reserva Las Gralarias, Ecuador, up to 2 inches. Status unknown.

[e] *Phyllobates terribilis* Endangered grows to about 2 inches.

Insects gone
Frogs gone
Fishes gone
Snakes gone
Mankind too soon gone
Mankind darn doggone!.

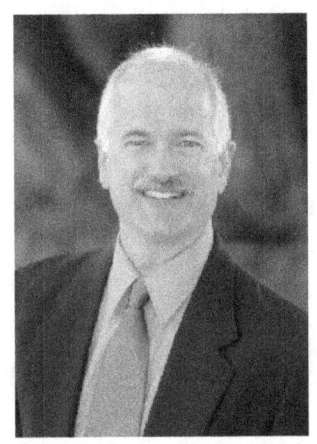

# JOHN GILBERT JACK LAYTON

He was born in Montreal in 1950
Was fluent in French and healthy
From proud father Robert Layton
To grand parent Gilbert Layton
Who too was dynamic and gung-ho
Who all held a ministerial portfolio
Raised as a true Canadian in Quebec in Hudson
Never dreamed of being a professor at Ryerson
In 1969 when he was just 19 yet he could afford
To marry high school sweetheart Sally Halford
With two kids Sally and Mike

He went to work riding a bike
He moved to Toronto and in Political Science got a PhD.
Not knowing cancer could snatch away his life so cruelly
He wasn't poor or rich
But he too got the itch
And he was a metro Councilor from 1982 up to 1988
Championing his cause putting all in the hands of fate
He remarried to the pretty Olivia Chow
She became an NDP MP in 2006, wow!
In 1990 Layton became of Toronto's Deputy Mayor
In 1997-2003 he settled down as a City Councillor
Failures for a Federal seat in winning he had a few
But gutsy Jack Layton had the Federal seat in view
He was the cork or bobbin which refused to sink
In 1919 he founded the Green Catalyst Group Inc.
And in 1993 he ran for the House of Commons and came in fourt'
But determined Jack Layton knew one day he would get the vote
In 2000 he published *Homelessness:*
*The Making and Unmaking of a Crisis*
He became the President in 2004 got the keys
Of the Canadian Federation of Municipalities
In 2003 became the Federal NDP Leader for sure
And was elected to the House of Commons in 2004
Later he was diagnosed with prostrate cancer
In 2011 he won 103 seats showed his stamina
He became Head of the Official Opposition Party
Then tragedy struck as he underwent hip surgery
He came out brave brandishing his cane
And we thought Jack was back once again
Then the strains showed still fighting his cancer

Vowed to defeat it and it was a battle very bitter
Then on August 22, 2011, his family got a bigger problem
For Jack Layton passed away at home that day at 4:45 am
Some called him *Citizen Jack* or *Gentleman Jack*
For the little people he was always on the attack
He fought for fairness and for compassion
Suffering silently as he did this in remission
Hard working with a fighting spirit
Alone Jack Layton did every bit of it
Fighting for the Homeless and the Environment
Trying to give gays and lesbians their equal vent
Even when his foes called him names like *Vladimir Jack*
*Taliban Jack* or *Chairman Jack* he gave them the slack
He never held any grudges he was above such petty jealousy
Fighting to build a United Canada yet he's all for democracy
In his final letter to Canadians he addressed us all
It was as if he knew it was going to be his last call
He said *Love is better than anger, Hope is better than fear*
*Optimism is better than despair so let us love show we care*
Not like some who are sheer apologies and pessimistic
*We'll change the world if we be hopeful and optimistic*
No other Politician except Pierre Trudeau
Showed such patriotism, charisma and glow
To be given such a well deserved State Funeral
Across Canada tears flowed from one and all
Who will show us that special human touch
The hugs and smiles we got to love so much
For his short 61 years on this beautiful world
John Gilbert Jack Layton gave it a real whirl
All politicians praised him for his good works

But why do they sometimes behave like jerks?
Denying the Social right for every child and senior
From our deserved wealth as our cup runneth over
Winning over 100 seats Jack made history
But his death left a hole in our Democracy
Why can't others from Jack's book take a page
Stop the puerile parliamentary sniping and rage
Put all Canadians first then look after the others
And stop the quagmire of hypocrisy my brothers!

# DUNCE

They answered *what?*
You just can't say that
Your words you have to select
For it's not politically correct
Long ago we say you are a dunce or crazy
Today it's *you're challenged intellectually*
When you don't pay attention
And have a 5yr old's retention
Can't say you have a disability either
Even if you are your brother's keeper
The so-called intellectuals would scoff
Then a good slap on the ears was enough
The beginning of all this modern crap
Started the day they deleted the strap
Now in class kids can take a snooze
You object all hell would break loose
Now they send you for psychiatry
All guided by the dumb Ministry
You can't even fail just copy your friend's at sup
Or they would changed the grades to move you up
Or wholesale anything from the computer

Or the nearby innocent looking wikipedia
Ask a student what's 12 x 9?
He'll sweat for all is not fine
He'll look like a deer caught in the headlight
Reaching for his calculator always in sight
No wonder they can't spell or count
But always ready to kiss or mount
For this is the new x- generation
Ready to party for any occasion

# YOU THINK YOU KNOW THEM

You think you know them
For living with them so long
But you have a big problem
You found out you're wrong

They came from your genes
Watching them romp in mirth
They left you as has-beens
Wondering about their birth

Then they've become men  and women
Hoping all is well without any downfall
You would see the real you but only when
Or not you may see the writing on the wall

Friends and families you have many
You gave them love with lullabies as they slept
Then they treat you like the enemy
Leaving you very cold as winter's windswept

In your job, or firm or working place
It maybe just because of your kith and kin

Some just hate you cause of your race
If it isn't race it's the colour of your skin

You really think you know them
But as grown ups you're so disappointed
And you also hate to condemn
Maybe thinking their heads got tainted

Our always forgiving country so awesome
Bending backwards with more barefaced demands
Trying to hold you down in a mental ransom
They seek our help, we stretched our weary hands

Then one day you woke up with folks around you
But you found out they have less love and or loyalty
As if you're fighting a losing battle no use to argue
Have we gone wrong! too numbed to even get angry

# THERE'S NO SUFFERING WITHOUT COMPASSION

Sometimes you look around at the suffering
Shake your head gradually and wondering
Why you allow this to happen my God!
Why wait why not bury me in the sod
Then I start to recollect the bad news
How Hitler murdered six million Jews
How does one retain one's sanity
In this darn dog eat dog society

The blacks and others had much suffering
From the hands of the whiteman's clouting
Segregation by Klu Klux Klan in the distant
Still today racial prejudice is very rampant
And yet they hypocritically work and pray
Together in the cities and ghettos very day
Today the suffering from white blackness
Because of the greed and the selfishness

Then I remember a long time ago
A very simple man with no show

Preached along the wayside
With 12 disciples at his side
He spoke of love for the brotherhood
He taught everything which was good
He expounded in his sagacious discussion
*Without suffering there's no compassion*

# IT'S BETTER TO BE ALONE

It is better to be alone in life's journey
Than to be in very evil bad company
When I see you and them in a car
I'll know who your real friends are
And if you run with the wolves
Don't get caught in the shelves
But if you soar with eagles
Find yourself in the jungles
You will learn how to soar to great heights
Experiencing some of life's simple delights
For a mirror reflects a man's face
Not tracking your running pace

You become like those with whom you  associate
Some may debate that you are like dead weight
Growing up you knew who's on a good card
And to grasp that was nothing so very hard
When you tolerate mediocrity in your drifters
You also lower your standard and that of others
An important attribute in all successful people is
When they dwell with positives they are in bliss
So learn to have a positive outlook in life

Teach and preach it to your kids and wife
And by that ma'm I mean vice versa
So if *he* is negative use your spatula

So we should all heed this one question
In order to heal and soothe our tension
What have become of our so-called modern society
We have been exposed to so much evil skulduggery
Where the poor folks always end up fetching the onuses
As the culprits get off with fat pensions and big bonuses
In sowing evil seeds what they did they knew
Got greedy and bit more than they can chew
Getting into hot water in the end
We don't think before we hit *send*
Using the social network bullying kids is another sore bone
I ask again maybe isn't it better to be lonesome and stay alone?

# THE HARD WAY IS THE ONLY WAY

The world's ever worst problems could be solved
Not drilling into kids what cannot be dissolved
Instead saying there are no short cuts and there's no free lunch
The hard way's the only way specially when you're in a crunch

We can't all be movie stars
We can't all be super stars
We can't all be stars someone has to mind the store
Someone has to do the dirtywork and that's for sure

Some of our kids have it too good
Whilst others just hold bare wood
They live in a fantasy world, their parents are always there
To bail them out of troubles so they are immune from fear

Gone are the days of daily chores or just a newspaper route
Helping the wretched homeless knowing what life is all about
Just doing good and not only in emergencies
Make it a way of life how to cope with crises

As my neice would say *Uncle this too shall pass*
Now its not only *eye-pass* its more like *rass-pass*

And life goes on the weak always pays the price
No one listens and no one will take my advice

But maybe I'm interfering with your constitutional strife
Or this isn't politically correct so I say, *Go! get a life*
 Clint would be able to tell all the gun lovers so unfit
*I say if there's a gun, I want to be in control of it.*

# WHAT HAPPENED TO THE FAMILY LIFE

The family table was always a happy time in eating
When the family caught up on the day's happening
Where manners were cultivated and accepted
Where rudeness and bad behavior were rejected
Here was where etiquette was ingrained
Daily adherence to this was maintained
Where kids say *please* and *thank you*
This was taken for granted nothing new
The kids who ate together behave better
Than their counterparts who were cruder

What happened to the head at the dining table
When life was harmoniously somewhat stable
Today we see the demise of the family dinner table
'cause Mom or Sister can't cook or they aren't able
She works full time and Sister works part time
One can get Mc Donald's or Wendy's anytime
The main meal of the day was dinner
Its irregularity today makes it supper
Everyone grabs something and heads for the TV
To watch *Two and a Half-Men* or *Judge Judy*

Dad once the head of the family laid down the law
He's replaced once by Cronkite now by Brokaw

Today we eat and run and go to work
To shop, to school and some go berserk
In the mornings its always hell with the brats
Breakfast time is full of *I don't want thats*
They don't want to eat their vegetables
Using all the excuses in all the angles
Maybe someone may eat their cereals
But they'll question the carbs and cals

Its a shame to think what progress can do to us
When spending a life time with beliefs we trus'
The Man and his taxmen have a blame here too
When folks are taxed to death without a clue
One can't cope to preserve a family anymore
It takes two plus and that's not even the cure
Parental love is snatched even from schoolwork
Kids rely on games, toys and every social jerk
Now they're too busy texting or playing games
As parents watch the decline of all their aims

# WORDS MAKETH THE MAN

Remember what the parrot parrot once said:
*The words we choose reveal our character*
Whether you be Hitler who said,
*If you tell a big enough lie and tell it frequently enough, it will be believed.*
Or JFk who shouted out, " *Ich bin ein Berliner"*
The wise East Indian Hindu Ghandi said it best with:
*An eye for an eye only ends up making the whole world blind.*
For those who got despondent with failures Bertrand Russell said:
*The time you enjoy wasting is not wasted time.*
Bertrand was wise enough to know
*Be kind whenever possible. It is always possible.*
Clint Eastwood would be able to tell all the gun lovers
*I have a very strict gun control policy, if there's a gun around, I want to be in control of it.*
Of all the great quotes the best came from Indians like Nehru
who said:
*Peace is not a relationship of nations.*
*It is a condition of mind brought about by a serenity of soul.*
*Peace is not merely the absence of war.*
*It is also a state of mind.*
*Lasting peace can come only to peaceful people*
Or Prem Rawat who said:

*Happiness is your own treasure because it lies within you.*
Or Bodhidharma who put it in a nutshell:
*The ignorant mind, with its infinite afflictions, passions, and evils, is rooted in the three poisons. Greed, anger, and delusion.*
At this festive time time Kinky Friedman said it best:
*Beauty is in the eye of the beer holder.*
And he continued with:
*I support gay marriage. I believe they have a right to be as miserable as the rest of us.*
But conclusively Sai Baba said it best:
*Life is a song - sing it.*
*Life is a game - play it.*
*Life is a challenge - meet it.*
*Life is a dream - realize it.*
*Life is a sacrifice - offer it.*
*Life is love - enjoy it.*
There are many more great men but space do not permit me to talk about them. However, I would be amiss if I don't quote Nelson Mandela who insisted;
*The roots of education are bitter, but the fruit is sweet.*
He also expounded:
*If you talk to a man in a language he understands, that goes to his head. If you talk to him in his own language, that goes to his heart."*
Abraham Lincoln said:
*Nearly all men can stand adversity, but if you want to test a man's character, give him power*
And William James countered with:
*If you can dream it, you can do it.*
Og Mandino says:

*Always do your best. What you plant now, you will harvest later.*

*What's money? A man is a success if he gets up in the morning and goes to bed at night and in between does what he wants to do.*

Charles Coburn:

*Marriage is like a business is easy to quit but you have to work hard to save it.*

And such wisdom can only come from the mouth of an angel, Mother Teresa who said,

*I have found the paradox, that if you love until it hurts, there can be no more hurt, only more love.*

*The Great* Nelson Mandela said;

*Education is the most powerful weapon which you can use to change the world.*

He continued:

*A good head and a good heart are always a formidable combination.*

When Winton Churchill met a woman who insulted him he remarked,

*I may be drunk, Miss, but in the morning I will be sober and you will still be ugly.*

The great Khalil Gibran spoke:

*The teacher who is indeed wise does not bid you to enter the house of his wisdom but rather leads you to the threshold of your mind.*

Elbert Hubbard said it right with:

*Do not take life too seriously. You will never get out of it alive.*

And Herb Caen added:

*A man begins cutting his wisdom teeth the first time he bites off more than he can chew.*

And this gem can only come from the sagacious genius Confucius:
*By three methods we may learn wisdom: First, by reflection, which is noblest; Second, by imitation, which is easiest; and third by experience, which is the bitterest.*
He continued:
*He who learns but does not think, is lost! He who thinks but does not learn is in great danger.*
And to that I add to all of them I say, ***Amen!***

*OTHER BOOKS BY*

# NARAINE DATT

*1)*   *A LONELY VOICE (50 Poems)*

*2)*   *DRINK FROM MY CALABASH (50 poems)*

*3)*   *RORAIMA ( 14 poems with 5 other poets)* Roop Misisr, Ram Jagessar, Habeeb Ali, Ken Rampahl and Harry Persaud.


**SOON TO BE PUBLISHED:**


(1) **A PORTRAIT IN VERSE.** *(50 Poems)*
(2) **HOW TO FIND YOUR PARTNER AND KEEP HER**
(3) **EL DORADO- THE CITY OF GOLD**
   *(HISTORY)*
(4) **THE BERBICIAN** *(NOVEL)*

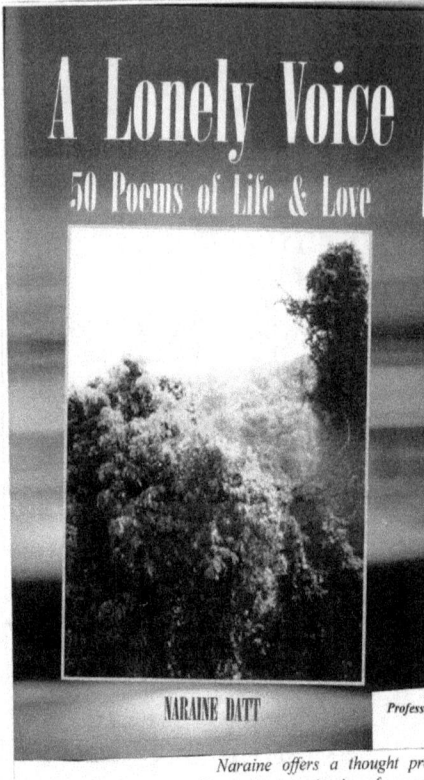

## 1)   *A LONELY VOICE (50 poems)*

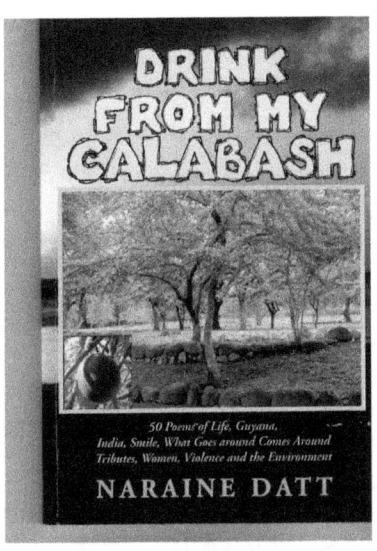

$18.00

2) *DRINK FROM MY CALABASH* *(50 poems)*

3) *RORAIMA (76 POEMS With Roop Misisr, Ram Jagessar,*

*Habeeb Ali, Ken Rampahl and Harry Persaud . ($15.00)*

4) GUYANA: STRATGIC PUBLIC POLICY.

Dr. Bertrand G Ramcharan. ($15.00)

**Also available:**

(5)  **A DIP AT THE SANGAM**

*Reuben Lachmansingh ($25.00)*

*(6)    LAYERS OF THE RAINFOREST*

*Shirley Najhram  ($8.00)*

**CONTACT: Naraine Datt (Norman)**

**EMAIL: ndatt@rogers.com**

*OR*

*CALL: (905) 420-2433*

*Paypal accepted.*

www.ingramcontent.com/pod-product-compliance
Lightning Source LLC
Chambersburg PA
CBHW051516170526
45165CB00002B/495